AMERICAN

HERITAGE

October 1957 · Volume VIII, Number 6

WE OWE ALLEGIANCE TO NO CROWN.

AMERICAN HERITAGE

The Magazine of History

PUBLISHER
James Parton

EDITORIAL DIRECTOR
Joseph J. Thorndike, Jr.

EDITOR
Bruce Catton

MANAGING EDITOR
Oliver Jensen

ASSOCIATE EDITOR
Richard M. Ketchum

ASSISTANT EDITOR
Joan Paterson Mills

EDITORIAL ASSISTANTS
Hilde Heun, Stephen W. Sears
Caroline Backlund, Lilyan Goldman
Art: Murray Belsky, Trudy Glucksberg

ART DIRECTOR
Irwin Glusker

ADVISORY BOARD
Allan Nevins, *Chairman*
Carl Carmer   Richard P. McCormick
Albert B. Corey   Harry Shaw Newman
Christopher Crittenden Howard H. Peckham
Marshall Davidson   S. K. Stevens
Louis C. Jones   Arthur M. Schlesinger, Sr.

REGIONAL EDITORS
Ray A. Billington.........*Evanston, Illinois*
John W. Caughey.....*Los Angeles, California*
K. Ross Toole.............*Helena, Montana*
Walter Prescott Webb........*Austin, Texas*

STAFF PHOTOGRAPHER
Herbert Loebel

CIRCULATION DIRECTOR
Richard V. Benson

AMERICAN HERITAGE is published every two months by American Heritage Publishing Co., Inc., 551 Fifth Avenue, New York 17, N. Y.
Single Copies: $2.95
Annual Subscriptions: $12.50 in the U.S.A.
$13.50 elsewhere

An annual Index of AMERICAN HERITAGE is published every February, priced at $1.00. AMERICAN HERITAGE is also indexed in *Reader's Guide to Periodical Literature.*

AMERICAN HERITAGE will consider but assumes no responsibility for unsolicited material. All such submissions should be accompanied by a stamped, self-addressed envelope.

Sponsored by
American Association for State & Local History · Society of American Historians

CONTENTS   *October 1957 · Volume VIII, Number 6*

COVERS: The heraldic stained glass panels of the Washington family which appear on the front and back covers are reproduced through the courtesy of the Corning Museum of Glass. For the story of these panels see "George Washington's Great-Great-Great-Great-Great-Grandfather slept here" on page 112.

FRONTISPIECE: This large and colorful patriotic composition was painted in the early 1800's by John A. Woodside of Philadelphia. It is owned by Robert C. Eldred of Cape Cod and was photographed through the courtesy of the Robert Carlen Gallery of Philadelphia.

Prescott's Conquests

By THOMAS F. McGANN

The great historian who so eloquently described the taking of Mexico and Peru won a great private victory of his own in the quiet of his study on Beacon Hill

"When you see Prescott, give him my cordial remembrances. You two are shelved together for immortality." Over a century ago Washington Irving thus prophesied an eternity of readers for two New England scholars, George Ticknor, first American master of European literature, and his close friend, the historian William H. Prescott. It is a coincidence of America's cultural flowering in the nineteenth century that three of its principal figures, Ticknor, Irving, and Prescott, should have been united by their devotion to the relatively unknown field of Spanish history and literature. Today, as Americans turn increasingly to rereading and revaluing their past and as the centenary of Prescott's death in 1859 approaches, it is fitting to examine his claim upon the reading public, to see whether or not it is still valid, and to measure his stature as man and historian.

With Irving, Prescott was the first American to devote profound study to the Hispanic world, our first historian of Spain and Latin America, those old yet new lands. He wrote two books of particular interest to all Americans, the *Conquest of Mexico*, which he published in 1843, and the *Conquest of Peru*, which appeared four years later. Both were immediate best sellers in the United States and England. The first, and expensive, three-volume edition of the *Conquest of Mexico* sold 4,000 copies in four months in the United

The illustration at the right, in which the original German heading has been replaced by a quotation from Prescott, is a title page in the monumental series of books on the Americas published between 1590 and 1634 by the famous family of Flemish engravers, the De Brys. This one shows the Inca Atahuallpa being carried on a litter and, below him, the Pizarro brothers landing in Peru in 1532. Around the sides appear scenes of gold mining well calculated to confirm the dreams and excite the avarice of the age. It was this spectacle of blood, greed, faith, and courage, equally mixed, of the clash of civilizations and the rise of empires, that three centuries later stirred to his depths the gentle, nearly blind Boston Brahmin at left, William Hickling Prescott.

The simple natives, with their defenceless bodies and rude weapons, were no match for the European warrior armed to the teeth in mail. The odds were as great as those found in any legend of chivalry, where the lance of the good knight overturned hundreds at a touch. The perils that lay in the discoverer's path, and the sufferings he had to sustain, were scarcely inferior to those that beset the knight-errant. . . . It was the reality of romance.

—Conquest of Peru

States. Both books were soon translated into several foreign languages.

There are good reasons for this early and continuing success, for each book is a brilliant account of the triumph of Spanish conquistadors over a rich, populous, and unknown Indian empire. Nor are all the courage and drama restricted to Prescott's printed pages. There was much in his own life, and to know the man behind the works is to understand one of the finest artistic and moral triumphs in American letters.

Prescott was semiblind. One of his eyes was almost totally sightless as the result of a college prank in which he was an innocent bystander. Soon after he suffered this wound his other eye was afflicted by a rheumatoid inflammation; during the rest of his life his vision with this eye wavered between good and painfully feeble. He had planned to become a lawyer, but this misfortune forced him to abandon that hope and, indeed, hope of any career. After his slow recovery from the physical and mental shocks caused by the double attack on his sight, Prescott did no more than devote himself to the life of an idle and well-to-do young gentleman. He was wealthy and he had a famous name (one of his grandfathers was a hero of the battle of Bunker Hill). He traveled a little, went out much in society, and read, within the limits of his sight and his desultory interests. In short, he drifted.

In 1824, when he was 28 years old, he began to plan a more fruitful future. Much influenced by Ticknor, who frequently read his Harvard lectures on Spanish literature to his half-blind friend, Prescott came to the conclusion that he had a vocation in literature, then narrowed this down to the writing of history—history then was closer to literature than it usually is today—and finally to Spanish history.

Once Prescott had made up his mind to enter the laborious discipline of history, he did not automatically become a historian. He next gave two years to general preparation for the work ahead. He read political theory and studied the languages, literature, and history of the major western European countries. Then followed ten years of specific historical work: organizing a technique for study, accumulating and reading all relevant documents and books, and finally writing his first book, *Ferdinand and Isabella*. During that decade there were not ten people in the city of Boston who knew that the affable and apparently indolent Prescott, who kept up his long daily horseback rides to Jamaica Pond and went out much in the evening, was writing a book which was to bring him national and international acclaim when it was published in 1837.

Fewer still knew the author's method of work. On

some days his eyes would stand two hours of reading, on others, not ten minutes. To absorb and shape the vast amount of historical data and ideas which he compressed into his books he invented his own technique.

When he had selected a theme for a chapter he had his secretary arrange all the materials which had been obtained. These were read to him, in itself a difficult operation, for Spanish was practically an unknown tongue in a city where French and German and Italian had not long since been considered outlandish, and Prescott was compelled to teach his successive readers and secretaries to pronounce the Spanish words of his books and manuscripts so that he could

Spaniard Against Spaniard

There is a kind of Homeric drama to Prescott's narratives, a quality well merited, of course, by the facts. An empire is stolen; the thieves fall out; Spaniard kills Spaniard. Thus the Conquest of Peru *ends with the suppression of the attempt of Gonzalo Pizarro, after his great brother Francisco's death, to make himself independent of the crown of Spain. The revolt was crushed by that great rarity, a man of virtue, Piedro de la Gasca, whom Prescott thought one of those men "specially designed by Providence" for great historic tasks. "Such was Washington in our own country," he adds, "and Gasca in Peru." But even at this high moment the venal aspects of human character appeared. Moved variously by greed and revenge, Gasca's lieutenants soon set upon members of the losing party (for example, Pedro de Puelles, in his bed, left) with dagger, spear, and garrote as the De Bry illustration here shows. As Prescott says: "We have seen sparkles of the chivalrous and romantic temper which belongs to the heroic age of Spain. But, with some honorable exceptions, it was the scum of her chivalry that resorted to Peru and took service under the banner of the Pizarros."*

understand them—so discouraging a task that more than once he thought of abandoning his chosen course. While the reading was in progress, Prescott sat with his back to the light (later he developed an intricate system of movable shades and drapes to direct and soften the daylight entering his study) taking notes on his noctograph. This was a frame crossed by guide wires and holding a sheet of carbon paper to be written on with a stylus. It obviated what Prescott termed "the two great difficulties in the way of a blind man's writing . . . his not knowing when the ink is exhausted in his pen, and when his lines run into one another."

The notes, often difficult to decipher from the uncertainty with which the letters and words were formed, were then copied by the secretary in a large hand. Prescott read the notes, if his eyes were up to it, or had the secretary read them as often as necessary for the author to fix them in his memory. Then he composed, wholly in his mind, for written drafts were luxuries which his sight would not permit. He concentrated and arranged and rearranged his thoughts into sentences, paragraphs, pages, until the chapter he was working on was formed in his mind as clearly as though in print.

Some chapters he thus mentally constructed and reconstituted as many as sixteen times; sometimes as many as sixty future printed pages were composed and gripped in his powerful mind—not only remarkable feats of memory but also superb achievements of artistic creation. Then he would begin to write on his noctograph, swiftly, exhausting the stored-up words. The finished work was read to him, corrected, copied by the secretary, and laid away for the printer.

If few knew Prescott's working habits, many knew the man about town. He was handsome, with a square jaw, a shock of curly brown hair, and a prominent, well-shaped nose which not only conformed to his other features but also to the local suspicion that in more than one way Boston's leaders resembled the Romans. Gay and kindly, generous with quietly given charity to the city's poor, immensely popular as a dinner companion, Prescott was devoted to his family and to his pattern of life: winter and spring in town, summer at the shore at Nahant and the beloved fall at

Pepperell, thirty miles northwest of Boston, at the family homestead standing on land held by the original Indian title.

Behind the affable exterior Prescott waged with himself a lifelong struggle. By disposition indolent, by inclination gregarious, he had a sufficiently large income to be free of the need to work. And his damaged vision afforded more than enough physical and psychological excuse for idleness.

His battle for self-mastery—a New England battle of conscience—is revealed in a combination of traits which form an odd counterpoint to his apparently harmonious character. He had a nervous laugh, often merely infectious, but sometimes uncontrollable, hysterical. He was a person of uncounted good resolutions, secret, childish goads to labor, resolutions verbally made or written down and sealed away, only to be broken, amended, reamended, and finally rescinded for a new set. He placed curious wagers on his ability to keep his resolutions, calling on a friend to make the bet against him but giving his opponent no infor-

mation as to what he was betting on. In due time Prescott would appear to pay or to collect the amount of the wager, leaving his friend no wiser, but a little richer or poorer.

The historian doted upon his parents, both of whom lived on into his middle life. He resided in their home even after his own marriage and, indeed, had no home of his own until his father died, when the younger Prescott was 48 years old. Nor did he have money of his own earning, being dependent upon the family income, although in later years his book royalties brought in a considerable sum. As his parents protected him, they also had to prod him. When the manuscript of his first book was ready for the printer, Prescott was stricken by fear of its inadequacy and of becoming the laughingstock of his circle. He did not release the manuscript until goaded by his father, who told him, "The man who writes a book which he is afraid to publish is a coward."

On the December day when his father was buried, as Prescott was closely following the bier into the

TEXT CONTINUED ON PAGE 109

Spaniard Against Indian

One of the high moments of Prescotts' Conquest of Peru, *shown on the facing page, is the capture in 1532 of the Inca Emperor Atahuallpa, who approached the Spaniards "elevated high above his vassals . . . on a sort of throne made of massive gold of inestimable value." Pizarro's chaplain stepped forward to expound the true faith, which, "by a curious chain of argument," linked the conquistadors to St. Peter. The doctrine of the Trinity suffered in translation, as the struggling interpreter explained that " 'the Christians believed in three Gods and one God, and that made four.' " Proud Atahuallpa contemptuously tossed the friar's Bible (or perhaps it was a breviary) to earth. " 'Set on, at once; I absolve you—' " cried the outraged priest. "Pizarro saw that the hour had come," says Prescott, and a dreadful slaughter began. The De Bry engraving, of course, is a fanciful depiction, like the other one below, which shows a tribe of Indians who dwelt in trees, supposedly first seen by Balboa, and who were very hard to conquer. Over half a century after these events, and working in faraway Frankfort on the Main, the De Brys did their best to dramatize the jumble of early and often fanciful accounts of explorations and battles across the sea. Long afterward the same materials came under the scrutiny of the more accurate and scrupulous Prescott, and the results have one great common denominator, for the ancient engraver and the Boston historian alike capture something almost beyond modern conception, the effect of the New World on the imagination of the Old.*

My Mouth Hurts
PRESIDENT GROVER CLEVELAND

When the

While panic gripped the nation i

House blocked that, the compromise Sherman Silver Purchase Act required the Treasury to buy 4,500,000 ounces of the white metal per month (the estimated total U.S. output), at market, and to issue notes against it redeemable either in silver or in gold. Most people, of course, took gold.

This was a particularly hazardous fiscal gesture at a time when European countries, and even Russia and India, had demonetized silver. The way foreigners queued up at his Treasury windows to get something for nothing gave Uncle Sam one of his early glimpses of himself as Uncle Sucker.

I'd Operate
DR. JOSEPH BRYANT

By putting on their ticket little Adlai E. Stevenson of Illinois, a former assistant postmaster general and a flirt with the Populist movement, the Democrats in 1892 were able to re-elect New York's trusted Grover Cleveland as President. No friend of soft money or Treasury raids, Cleveland had stood against both in his 1884-88 term, and he still maintained his opposition. But even before he retook office, the earthquake was in motion and much of the havoc wrought.

W hen Charles Francis Adams called what happened to the United States in 1893 its "most deep-seated financial storm," his metaphor was weak. More than a storm, it was a major earthquake, a violent onset of national growing pains which upheaved the young country's financial crust and shook the whole continental economy along major fault lines.

The Republicans' high protective tariffs had put fat gold surpluses into the Treasury which not even Republican largess to Civil War pensioners depleted. But the tariffs and gold were no good for farmers, just then in a run of their leanest years. Despairing for cheaper money and more of it, the westerners turned to silver, of which some of the new states just admitted to the Union had mountains at bargain prices. In 1890 their senators very nearly obtained the free and unlimited coinage of silver. When the Republican-controlled

Cancer, Definitely
DR. WILLIAM H. WELCH

More than $100 million in silver notes had been issued, redeemable in gold. The gold reserve was down from $185 million to $101 million and was soon to fall lower yet. That winter and spring of 1893, the Treasury was kept solvent only by omitting sinking fund payments and not spending appropriations voted by Congress.

The clang of closing bank doors reverberated through the land; 642 would shut this year. Savings banks required thirty days notice for withdrawals. Call money was 60 per cent in March and headed for 73 per cent. In February the solid old Reading Railroad went into receivership.

President Disappeared

1893, Grover Cleveland suffered his own secret ordeal on a yacht in Long Island Sound

By JOHN STUART MARTIN

As unemployment spread, not only did panic grip industrialists and financiers, but stark desperation and actual starvation gripped the working masses. Not for another year would Coxey's Army march on the White House, but Grover Cleveland could already hear it being recruited. His solid sense was sickened, and his honest heart.

The whole trouble, he saw, was the Silver Act, which only he might be able to get Congress to repeal. When it failed to do so before recessing in June, President Cleveland, on that month's last day, issued a call for a special session to convene on August 7, to save the nation's fiscal health and sanity.

Those two dates in black 1893—June 30 and August 7—are worth closer scrutiny. Between them lay an act of personal courage and determination unparalleled in the annals of our Presidents.

For on June 30, at as dark an hour as his country had ever known, the President of the United States disappeared entirely. He did so for a dire reason which was national as well as personal. As he saw it, both he and his country were in sight of the gates of death, and only by a lonely act of his could these be avoided.

On June 18, gruffly as was his wont, Grover Cleveland had asked Dr. Robert M. O'Reilly, the White House physician, to have a look at a "rough place" in the roof of his cigar-chewing mouth. It had, he said, been bothering him for a matter of weeks and felt worse all the time.

What O'Reilly saw was an angrily inflamed area about the size of a silver quarter, extending out to the median line from the left bicuspids and back to the soft palate. He took tissue samples and sent them anonymously to the Army Medical Museum and also to the country's top pathologist, Dr. William H. Welch at Johns Hopkins.

Cigar-chewing, whisky-drinking Ulysses Grant had lately died, slowly and painfully, of a neglected mouth cancer. Thus O'Reilly and Cleveland were shocked but not exactly surprised when the pathologists' reports concurred in one horrid word: "Malignant."

Cleveland's instant reply to this news was one other word: "Secrecy." The already shaken country must not know.

A hurried visit to Washington by his great and good friend Dr. Joseph Bryant of New York aroused no suspicions. These two were hunting and fishing cronies as well as doctor and patient. But when Joe Bryant, after confirming the diagnosis, told him, "Were it in my mouth, I would have it removed at once!" Grover Cleveland had to cogitate, to plot and plan. He did so almost instantly and with forthright resolution. Calling in Dan Lamont, his former press secretary, now his secretary of war, he concerted with Bryant for an operation on July 1, under conditions as cleverly contrived as they were critical.

Keep It Secret
ADVISER
DANIEL LAMONT

Take My Yacht
COMMODORE
ELIAS C. BENEDICT

Waiting at Home
YOUNG MRS. CLEVELAND

A few minutes after issuing his call to Congress for a date only six weeks beyond his private ordeal, Grover Cleveland left the White House with Dan Lamont and Dr. Bryant in the afternoon of June 30. They boarded the 4:20 northbound train. (There were no detectives, for secret service men were not assigned as regular presidential guards until after McKinley's assassination in 1901.) The press was not told that he was leaving. The story would be, if his move were discovered, that he was just slipping away to rest at Gray Gables, his summer home on Buzzard's Bay, where his young and again pregnant wife had gone already.

Unnoticed in the dusk, the President left his train at New York and with Dr. Bryant went from the station to the Battery in a common carriage. Dim in the night offshore lay Commodore Elias C. Benedict's graceful yacht *Oneida*. Her tender quietly ferried the President of the United States out to and aboard her, unseen, unsuspected.

Interested Party
VICE PRESIDENT
ADLAI E. STEVENSON

The tender had already made a few other such unobtrusive trips that afternoon and evening. At casually spaced intervals it had fetched Dr. O'Reilly; Dr. Edward G. Janeway, the country's foremost physiologist; Dr. William W. Keen of Philadelphia, an oral surgeon of highest repute; Dr. Bryant's brilliant young assistant, Dr. John F. Erdmann (who was to succeed him as "top knife" of New York for a long span of years); and a Dr. Ferdinand Hasbrouck of 147 West 126th Street, Manhattan. No surgical bigwig, the latter was a young dentist, but urgently required by the others for his knowledge of the new "laughing gas," nitrous oxide, for anesthesia.

The dumpy but distinguished patient greeted all these gentlemen tersely and sat with them a while on deck, smoking one more cigar. He did not discuss his ugly ailment but did growl, "Oh, those office seekers! They haunt me even in my dreams!"

About midnight Dan Lamont and Joe Bryant went to their Manhattan homes to sleep, returning before the first sun of July had burned the mist off Manhattan's rivers. The *Oneida* sailed betimes, moving up the East River and out through Hell Gate into a glassy Long Island Sound, with Commodore Benedict and Dan Lamont plainly in evidence on deck to make it look to any curious eyes on shore like an ordinary rich man's pleasure cruise over the Fourth. Inside the yacht's main saloon the scene was far less usual.

This space, with wide overhead transoms, had been fitted up as a floating surgery. A straight-back chair was lashed to the mast to receive the patient. Sheeted paraphernalia were ranged about, including besides Dr. Hasbrouck's gas machine a standard ether-giving rig, a manually operated generator for magneto-cautery, tables of instruments for surgeons Bryant and Keen, and a chair beside the patient's for Dr. Janeway, who would check pulse, blood pressure, and respiration throughout the hacking and scraping. The yacht's steward was put into a surgical gown so that he could function as orderly. Boiling water and cracked ice were on hand in good supply.

Several times during the morning Cleveland's mouth was washed out and disinfected. Shortly before noon he was led pajamaed from his stateroom to the chair and there strapped in, head tilted back as though for a shave.

Dr. Bryant, in charge of everything, nodded to Dr. Hasbrouck for the gassing to begin. The importance of this part was that, deep under heavy ether, oral patients might choke to death on their own blood. From the lighter gas they could more easily be aroused to cough it up. Moreover, Cleveland was precisely the overweight, hypertensive type to go into an apoplexy if he choked at all.

Cleveland went under the gas readily, and the skillful Hasbrouck, with heavy forceps, swiftly extracted two bicuspids to make room for the surgeons' work. Now came the moment for Dr. Keen's specialty. From Paris he had lately brought back an ingenious cheek retractor, which would give Joe Bryant's strong big fingers free play without a hole being cut through the face.

Into the posterior dental ridge now bared by this instrument, Joe Bryant grimly carved with his white-hot electric knife, excising with it a section of the mouth's roof out to the midline and back to an apparently affected portion of the palate. His great concern was not to invade the orbital palate, that is, eye socket.

The Leak, Denied
REPORTER
E. J. EDWARDS

**Years Later,
The Truth**
DR. WILLIAM W. KEEN

BROWN BROTHERS

12

When Bryant was about half through cutting, Dr. Hasbrouck warned that the gas would soon wear off and the patient awaken. So at 1:14 Dr. O'Reilly administered ether and presently Dr. Bryant resumed his work.

When Cleveland's left antrum was fully exposed, it was seen to be filled with "a soft, gray, gelatinous mass"—the lethal sarcoma. Scooping and scraping this away, Dr. Bryant pared the excavation's limits to remove as many wild fringe cells as possible.

Bleeding was kept to a fortunate minimum—only about six ounces (one tumblerful). What with hot water, ice packs, pressure, and the cauterizing effect of the heated blade, they had to tie off only one blood vessel. Before 2 p.m. all was finished, the cavity stuffed with gauze, the patient back in bed. When he started coming to, about three o'clock, they gave him one-sixth of a grain of morphine. Pulse, blood pressure, and temperature all behaved well, the latter at no time rising above 100.8 degrees.

While the President slept, all hands took a stiff drink and a late lunch. In their vigils that night they knew what no one else in America or the world knew: that the President of the United States had, with their aid, confronted a mortal enemy and, in all likelihood, defeated it for himself and his nation in silence.

Late the next afternoon, July 2, Cleveland felt well enough to leave his bed and walk around a bit. His spirit matched his iron constitution, and through the packings in his mouth he did not complain but thanked those who came in turn to read to him.

He was not told about a difficulty that had arisen with Dr. Hasbrouck. As soon as his job was done the first day, this gentleman asked to be set ashore. The others firmly declined. To go in now might jeopardize their tremendous secret, and besides there might be complications such as hemorrhaging, with more gas needed. But by the afternoon of July 2 Hasbrouck was frantic as well as disgruntled. He was, he said, 48 hours late for another critical operation. Now the rest relented, and the tender put Dr. Hasbrouck ashore at New London.

On July 3 Cleveland was up and around all day. He belatedly signed the ship's register with a hand that was quick and firm.

On July 4 the *Oneida* ran in to Sag Harbor, where Dr. Keen was put ashore.

Late in the afternoon of the fifth, the *Oneida* moored in Buzzard's Bay and a squat, limping figure wrapped in a cloak made his way up the private dock at Gray Gables. The world was told that he had been treated for two ulcerated teeth and a recurrence of his pedal rheumatism. While he went to bed, his friends

mounted guard, Joe Bryant not far from bedside, Dan Lamont to cope with a hornets' nest.

At nearby Buzzard's Bay village, the gentlemen of the nation's press had been kicking their heels for five full days and nights with no word of any kind as to their President's whereabouts. When the *Oneida* was sighted offshore, fretfulness became fury which Lamont confronted in an old gray barn on the Cleveland estate. With a smoothness to match anything later displayed by a Steve Early or a Jim Hagerty, Dan Lamont gave them the rheumatism routine and expressed hurt dismay at all questions probing for a "malignancy," a mortal illness. He sent the reporters away silenced if not mollified, but they were back again the next day with a fresh line of attack.

Vice President Stevenson, they said, had heard the President's condition was so serious that he was entraining at once from New York to come up and investigate. Dan Lamont squelched this move by announcing that Mr. Stevenson was neither invited to nor expected at Gray Gables.

In view of Stevenson's cahooting with the Silverites and his influence in the Senate, a hard-money New York columnist cracked: "The Buzzards will please keep aloof from Buzzard's Bay!"

So no "buzzard" came, but on July 7 the President's devoted friend and favorite actor, Joe Jefferson, came, cheering him vastly. And Dan Lamont and Joe Bryant stayed on, the latter taking Cleveland out, as was their custom, to fish for stripers and drumfish from a rowboat, where the salt air was as good therapy as any. An orthodontist, Dr. Kasson C. Gibson was brought

CONTINUED ON PAGE 102

The Scene Itself, THE YACHT *Oneida*

Heyday of the
FLOATING PALACE

By LEONARD V. HUBER

Nicholas Roosevelt's fire canoe transformed the Mississippi

More than 270 years had slipped by since Hernando de Soto first stumbled onto the Mississippi, and in all that time the river had been host to an increasing variety of boats. For longer than anyone could reckon, the sleek canoes of the Indian had been there, but slowly and almost imperceptibly they began to be outnumbered by the arks, keelboats, and flatboats of the white man, laden with furs and less romantic cargoes, making the lazy trip down river.

Neither the river nor the people watching from its banks had ever seen anything quite like the bizarre craft which hove into sight in the year 1811. And there is good reason to doubt if any boat, before or since, had such a journey— a Homeric trip on which anything might happen, and nearly everything did. This was the maiden voyage of the *New Orleans,* the first steamer on the Mississippi River.

The story of steamboating in western waters began less than two weeks after Robert Fulton's *Clermont* made her successful trip up the Hudson in 1807, when Fulton made inquiries about the Mississippi. Successful in obtaining a monopoly on steamboat operation in New York, he and Chancellor Livingston were able to acquire the same rights from the Territory of Orleans—later Louisiana. In 1809 they sent Nicholas Roosevelt, brother of Theodore Roosevelt's great-grandfather Jacobus, to Pittsburgh with instructions to survey the rivers. Traveling aboard a flatboat, Roosevelt and his wife, Lydia, daughter of architect Benjamin Latrobe, floated downstream, asking questions, observing, taking soundings, and spotting

Five o'clock was the departure time of many steamboats, and an afternoon scene on the New Orleans levee was just as busy as the painting at left, by French artist Hyppolite Sebron, makes it out to be. Above, an early steamboat with sails passes New Orleans' Place d'Armes.

15

In 1855 Currier & Ives published this print of the steamboat Mayflower, *which made the trip between St. Louis and New Orleans. Three-dollar bills like the one below served as currency along the Mississippi. This one bears on its face a view of Lawrence, Kansas, where it was issued about 1860.*

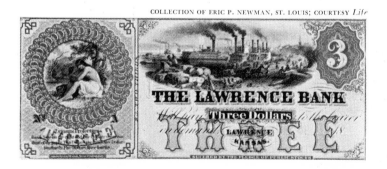

coal mines along the route for possible future use. Along the way, Roosevelt's talk of a boat that could travel up as well as downstream was greeted with laughter or polite disbelief, but after he made his report to Fulton and Livingston the backers decided to go ahead at once.

Construction began at Beelen's iron foundry, below Boyd's Hill in Pittsburgh, in the spring of 1811, and despite floods on the Monongahela which threatened to carry everything downstream prematurely, the *New Orleans* was launched in September. Built according to Fulton's plans, the boat was 148 feet long, powered by a Boulton & Watt "steeple" engine with a 34-inch cylinder which developed less than 100 horsepower. The blue-hulled vessel carried two masts and, with its elaborately furnished cabins, cost $38,000—quite a sum in those days. A few old sketches and woodcuts of the *New Orleans* survive, some showing her as a side-wheeler, others as a stern-wheeler, but most authorities believe that she was, like Fulton's *Clermont*, a side-wheeler. Captain Henry Shreve, who broke the Fulton-Livingston monopoly, built the stern-wheelers which

were prototypes for the western riverboats. The local citizenry considered this strange craft itself folly enough for one man, but when they heard that Mrs. Roosevelt—quite obviously pregnant—was accompanying her husband on his first voyage, they were convinced of his madness. All this served to heighten the excitement as the *New Orleans* finally slipped out into the stream, leaving a waving, shouting crowd behind as she headed into the Ohio.

Aboard, in the two cabins, were Mr. and Mrs. Roosevelt, the captain, an engineer named Baker, Andrew Jack the pilot, six hands, two female servants, a steward, a cook, and an enormous Newfoundland dog named Tiger. Past a shore line of limitless forest, broken occasionally by clearings where startled onlookers appeared to see and cheer them, they pushed downstream for two days at a speed of eight to ten miles an hour—"as jolly a set as ever floated on the Ohio." Anchoring at Cincinnati, they were greeted by the mayor, who congratulated Roosevelt on his achievement, but added somewhat sorrowfully:

". . . we see you for the last time. Your boat may go *down* the river, but as to coming up, the very idea is an absurd one."

The *New Orleans* dropped anchor at Louisville on October 1, 1811, a bright moonlit night. Although it was late, crowds assembled at the riverbank, some of them convinced that the loud hissing noise they heard was caused by the comet of 1811 falling into the Ohio. During several days ashore, Roosevelt first received congratulations from everyone he met, then their condolences that this was the first and last time a steamboat would be seen above the Falls of the Ohio, the dangerous rapids in the river at Louisville. To convince them otherwise, Roosevelt invited some of his hosts aboard, and while they were at dinner the boat got under way. There was a rush to the upper deck, where the passengers discovered to their utter astonishment that they were actually moving upstream. After going up river for a few miles, the *New Orleans* and the delighted guests returned to the original anchorage.

Now began the series of events which makes most

The fire which burned the steamboat Ruth *in 1863 was said to have been set by a southern sympathizer.*

This photograph of Captain Cooley's Ouachita, *taken in 1892, shows her "loaded to the guards" with cotton.*

All of the later steamboats had ornate interiors, but the cabin of the Grand Republic *outdid most of them.*

later steamboat voyages pale by comparison. There was not, at the time, enough water in the river to permit the *New Orleans* to negotiate the Falls of the Ohio, and Roosevelt had to wait for a rise in the stream. The outlook was far from promising. Each day dawned dull and misty with a cloudless sky and a strange overpowering atmosphere. Most ominous was the sun, which looked for all the world like "a globe of red hot iron," with a lack of brilliance that enabled watchers to stare at it without turning away. On one of these hot, still days Mrs. Roosevelt gave birth to her baby, and finally, in the last week of November, the river rose to a point where the falls were five inches more than the draft of the *New Orleans*. It was a tight squeeze, but Roosevelt decided to attempt the passage.

Steerage way and navigation of the vessel depended on its speed exceeding that of the current, and they put on all the steam the boiler would stand. With safety valve shrieking, the *New Orleans* practically leaped away from the crowds assembled to witness her departure, and as she headed into white water everyone on board reached instinctively for something solid to hold onto. No one spoke a word. The tense pilots directed the helmsman by motions of their hands until, after what must have seemed like hours, the *New Orleans* rounded to safety below the falls.

While she lay there at anchor, the passengers became aware of a strange motion. The anchor cable shook and trembled, almost as if the boat had been moving and then, suddenly, had run aground. Several of them were affected with nausea, and the vessel's movement became more pronounced as the series of shocks continued throughout the night. Violent earthquakes, particularly severe in the Mississippi Valley, had followed the comet of 1811, and the party aboard the *New Orleans* had run right into them.

Next day, moving down river, they were pursued by Chickasaw Indians in a canoe. They outran them easily, but when Roosevelt was awakened that night by shouts and trampling feet on the deck, he grabbed for a sword, thinking they had attacked again. Hurrying from the cabin with sword in hand, he discovered that the *New Orleans* was on fire, and not until a good part of the forward cabin had been destroyed was the blaze put out.

As they moved down the Mississippi, the travelers were greeted at each landing by victims of the "days of horror"—the terrible earthquakes which had devastated this land. At New Madrid, terrified inhabitants begged to be taken aboard, but there was simply not enough room for them. As J. H. B. Latrobe, writing some years later of his sister's voyage, said: "One of the peculiar characteristics of the voyage was the

"Wooding-up": the early steamboats consumed enormous quantities of firewood which was replenished en route at riverside wood yards. Roustabouts and deck passengers carried it aboard.

silence that prevailed on board. No one seemed disposed to talk. . . . Tiger . . . prowled about, moaning and growling. . . . Orders were given in low tones, and the usual cheerful 'aye, aye, sir,' of the sailors was almost inaudible. Sleeplessness was another characteristic." While they were ashore, gathering wood or coal, the men would wait while the earth shook, staring at each other until it ceased. Instead of calling greetings to them, the crews of barges and flatboats passed by silently, almost sullenly. Mrs. Roosevelt recorded that she "lived in constant fright, unable to sleep or sew or read."

To the Indians they met, who called the steamboat "Penelore" or "fire canoe," the *New Orleans* was an omen of evil. Sparks from its chimney were related to the comet which preceded the earthquake, and the revolving paddles to the rumbling of the earth. So great were the changes in the channel that the pilot lost his way; where he expected deep water, roots and stumps appeared above the surface. Tall trees once used as markers had disappeared, islands had changed shape. And once when the boat was made fast for the night to an island bank, the passengers awoke next morning to find that the island had disappeared.

As the *New Orleans* descended the river she left behind the earthquake area, but two more incidents were to round out the saga of this first Mississippi steamboat voyage. The first occurred in front of thou-

Lloyd's Steamboat Directory, 1856

sands of onlookers at Natchez when, as the *New Orleans* was rounding to for a landing, her head of steam gave out and she started drifting downstream with the current. At the last moment, the engineer got up enough steam to work the vessel into shore. The final episode was a happy one, as befitted a saga of this kind. As J. H. B. Latrobe relates it, the captain had fallen in love with Lydia Roosevelt's maid, ". . . prosecuted his suit so successfully as to find himself an accepted lover when the *New Orleans* reached Natchez, and a clergyman being sent for, a wedding marked the arrival of the boat at the chief city of Mississippi."

The age of steam on the western rivers began with the *New Orleans*, and Fulton and Livingston followed up their first success with the *Vesuvius*, the *Aetna*, the *Buffalo*, and a second *New Orleans* after the original was impaled on a stump and sank. But bad luck dogged their operations and they were never able to capitalize on their initial advantage. Meanwhile a group of men at Brownsville, Pennsylvania, some fifty miles up the Monongahela River from Pittsburgh, had built and were operating steamboats without benefit of licensing. Both Daniel French and Henry M. Shreve of the Brownsville group contributed much to early steamboat design, particularly

This woodcut sketch of the first New Orleans *(above) was made about forty years after her historic voyage and inaccurately shows her as a stern-wheeler. Most of the ingredients which constitute the popular, romantic conception of life as it once was along the great river are included in the Currier & Ives lithograph below, entitled* Low Water in the Mississippi. *On the facing page another Currier & Ives print depicts a steamboat moving through a moss-hung Louisiana bayou at night. In order to illuminate the overhanging trees bordering this tortuous stream, flaming torch-baskets have been installed on either side of the guards.*

Shreve, who brought out the *Washington* in 1816, the biggest steamboat yet built. After 1818, when the Fulton-Livingston monopoly was virtually dead, more and more builders came into the field.

Fifty-five years later there were several hundred boats, large and small, operating out of New Orleans. It was possible to book passage on one of 41 lines to Pittsburgh, Cincinnati, Louisville, St. Louis, Vicksburg, Nashville, Florence, Shreveport, and Jefferson, to say nothing of countless places on tributary streams. Yet 110 years after Nicholas Roosevelt's voyage, New Orleans newspapers carried the advertisement of just one steamboat and the great era was dead. It had lasted a little over a century—years in which steamboating and New Orleans became a legend together. And when the steamboat vanished, New Orleans' commercial prestige was to wane for many years.

By trial and error, the early steamboat builders gradually improved the vessels. The ocean-ship characteristics of the first boats with their deep-rounded hulls, masts for sails, and bowsprits gradually disappeared. Hulls were made shallower so that the boats rode *on* the water instead of *in* it; bowsprits made way for the jack staff, a tall flagpole on the bow which had great value to the pilot in sighting his course. The first engines—cumbersome vertical affairs—were super-seded by machines with stationary horizontal cylinders and oscillating pitmans which drove the paddle wheels. Since the hulls were quite shallow, boilers and engines were placed *on* the main deck and a second (and eventually a third or texas deck) was added for the accommodation of passengers. This revolution in design produced a type of boat which was to become characteristic of all steamboats on the Mississippi and its tributaries. During the first two decades after Roosevelt's *New Orleans*, 269 boats were built; but between 1830 and 1840 the demand for more and more resulted in the construction—mostly at Pittsburgh, Cincinnati, Louisville—of some 729 vessels.

Specialization soon entered into steamboat construction. Some firms built hulls, others engines, still others cabins. And for nearly half a century, steamboats were built by craftsmen using rule-of-thumb methods without plans. A captain would journey to Jeffersonville or New Albany and simply tell his boatbuilder what he wanted—"a twenty-five hundred bale boat—so wide, so long, so many boilers, so many staterooms"—and the result was usually to his satisfaction. In later years, plans were used; but such famous boats as the *Natchez* and the *Rob't E. Lee* were built without them.

Since the low flat hull was so little in evidence, the designer-builders concentrated their efforts above the

No one really believed the notices Captains Cannon and Leathers published in the Daily Picayune (below). On June 30, 1870, when the Rob't E. Lee and the Natchez left New Orleans within three minutes of each other, ten thousand people crowded the wharf, bets were made on the other side of the Atlantic, and millions of dollars eventually changed hands over the contest between these evenly matched rivals.

Actually, the race was never as close as this lithograph would indicate. By the time the Natchez passed Baton Rouge, the Lee was nine miles in the lead and reached St. Louis over six hours ahead of the Natchez. The Lee carried no freight, but Captain T. P. Leathers (below) accepted a full passenger and freight load. Although his Natchez lost the race, he had a net profit of four thousand dollars to console him.

A CARD TO THE PUBLIC.

Being satisfied that the steamer NATCHEZ has a reputation of being fast, I take this method of informing the public that the reports of the Natchez leaving here next Thursday, the 30th inst:, intending racing, are not true.

All passengers and shippers can rest assured that the Natchez will not race with any boat that may leave here on the same day with her. All business entrusted to my care, either in freight or passengers, will have the best attention. T. P. LEATHERS,

Je25—5t2dp   Master Steamer Natchez.

A. CARD.

Reports having been circulated that steamer R. E. LEE, leaving for Louisville on the 30th June, is going out for a race, such reports are not true, and the traveling community are assured that every attention will be given to the safety and comfort of passengers.

The running and management of the Lee wil in no manner be affected by the departure o other boats.

Je19—ot2dp   JOHN W. CANNON, Master

water line. With great resourcefulness, they evolved a new architectural form combining the great, ugly, and bulky paddleboxes, the towering chimneys, and the sprawling superstructure into a graceful type of vessel which seemed to rest securely on the water rather than to tower awkwardly above it.

The cabin builders were chiefly responsible for bringing to full flower the "floating palace" tradition, an elegance which bordered on magnificence. On the larger boats, the cabin, 200 feet long or more, was a "long resplendent tunnel" separating staterooms and serving as social hall and dining room for the passengers. Elaborately carved brackets supported ceilings frequently covered with a riot of near-Gothic ornament. Light from stained glass clerestory windows fell on varicolored Brussels carpets often woven especially for the boat; imported chandeliers, paintings, rich draperies, plush-covered furniture, and that ultimate of Victorian elegance, the grand piano, were reflected in the towering, gleaming mirror at the end of the ladies cabin. This was travel in style!

By 1850 the Mississippi River steamboat had reached the acme of design. No important structural changes took place after that except that builders made some of their boats much bigger and generally yielded to the popular taste that marked the sixties and seventies by providing an exuberance of gingerbread decoration. These embellishments earned the steamboat the derisive characterization of "Engine on a raft with $11,000 worth of jig-saw work around it."

In mid-century the building and repair of steamboats was a major industry of the western country. Six thousand steamboats of more than a million tons in aggregate were built and run on the Mississippi and its tributaries from 1820 to 1880.

From the earliest days, steamboat operation was plagued by boiler explosions. The tenth boat to be built, Shreve's *Washington*, exploded on her maiden voyage in June, 1816, the first of a long series of such disasters which, next to racing, became the most notable feature of the steamboat legend. By 1850 some 185 boats had blown up with a loss of life exceeding 1,400. One of the most spectacular of these occurred in 1849 when the *Louisiana* exploded at the levee in New Orleans. Two boats lying next to her were leveled to the water and the force of the explosion carried a heavy piece of metal five city blocks. The *Louisiana* sank within ten minutes and some 86 persons lost their lives.

Of all the explosions on the river, the worst took place in April, 1865, when the steamer *Sultana* [see AMERICAN HERITAGE, October, 1955] picked up 2,400 returning Union prisoners of war at Vicksburg and crowded them with 180 civilian passengers and crew

The meals aboard the M.S. Mepham *were as elaborate as its bill of fare, which included two dozen imported wines.*

onto a boat designed to hold one-sixth of that number. In the middle of the night, a few miles above Memphis, a boiler exploded and the *Sultana* caught fire. It was a rainy night; the Mississippi was at flood stage and three miles wide. Many were killed by burning and drowning. The official count of the dead and missing in this disaster was 1,547—more than were lost on the *Titanic*.

Other accidents took their toll. Snaggings—running

into heavy sticks of timber implanted in the bottom of the river—caused many a sinking. Collisions—the result of careless or negligent operations, especially at night—were not uncommon. Next to explosions, fire was the most dreaded hazard. The boats were made of wood and there was a constant danger of flying sparks from furnaces and chimneys. In 1837 the *Ben Sherrod* was on a trip from New Orleans to Louisville. Trying to overtake a rival, the captain of the *Sherrod* ordered the fireman to pile on fuel. The boilers became overheated and set fire to sixty cords of pine wood stacked too close for safety, and in a matter of minutes the boat was a flaming torch. The fire set off a barrel of whisky, the boilers exploded, and finally some forty barrels of gunpowder let go. Of the 200 passengers aboard the *Sherrod*, 72 perished. Other steamboats were nearby, and some picked up survivors; but one, the *Alton*, steaming to the rescue, only succeeded in plowing through the hapless victims in the water.

A man named Cook, a passenger from the *Sherrod*, managed with some other survivors to grasp a floating object. As they were being carried downstream, they saw a man standing on shore, hailed him, and implored his help; soon he came out into the river in a small boat looking for baggage and boxes in the debris of the wreck. When he came close, the man asked with the utmost *sang-froid*, "How much will you give me?" When he was not satisfied by what was offered, he paddled off, saying, "Oh, you're well off there; keep cool and you'll come out comfortable."

But there were lighter sides to steamboating, too. Nearly every boat was sooner or later given a nickname by the cheerful, carefree roustabouts who carried the freight on board and off on their shoulder bones. Quick to seize on some characteristic of the boat, the Negroes came up with some fantastic titles. For instance they called the *Ouachita*—"Oyster Loaf," *Danube*—"You be dam," *Paul Tulane*—"Two days and a half," *Richmond*—"Rebel Home," *G. W. Sentell*—"Broken Back," *Mabel Comeaux*—"Fuss Maker," and *Wheelock*, probably because of the scant quantity of food served them—"Starvation."

The boats themselves were often given intriguing names, like *Silver Heels, Swan, Starlight, Dew Drop, Fawn, Lotus, Swamp Fox, Grand Turk*. Captain E. Parker, master of the packet *Piota*, called his boat by that name because the letters stood for "Parker is obliged to all."

The men who ran them were as distinctive a breed as the boats. The most picturesque character aboard was generally the mate. He had one of the most demanding jobs—down on the main deck with the freight, the deck passengers, and the rousters. His temper and vocabulary were legendary; he had to be tough and he had to know how to handle Negroes, for roustabouts respected and would work well for a mate who understood them, even though he might be stern and take a stick of wood to them on occasion.

COLLECTION OF STRATFORD LEE MORTON, ST. LOUIS

The engineer had the hot and sweaty job of keeping the engines going, often for days at a time without the opportunity to make repairs. The engineer was almost certain to pay with his life if he made a serious error in judgment with his boilers and his engine. Generally, the engineer was taken for granted; nobody thought much about him except during races or in case of disaster when he was the first to be blamed —that is, if he was still around. The striker was his assistant.

The clerk was business manager and freight and passenger agent. He purchased fuel and supplies, hired and fired the lesser crew members, assigned passengers their quarters.

The assistant clerk was known as the "mud clerk," a name derived from the muddy feet he got at landings, receiving and delivering freight in all sorts of weather.

The pilot, immortalized by Mark Twain, had to know every bend, every snag, and every sand bar along the way, by night and by day, in clear weather or in foul. In his lofty aerie atop the texas, encased in glass with a commanding view of the river; with bell-pulls and a speaking tube to convey his orders to the engi-

CONTINUED ON PAGE 96

The Sergeant Major's

General Washington wanted Benedict Arnold taken alive, right in the heart

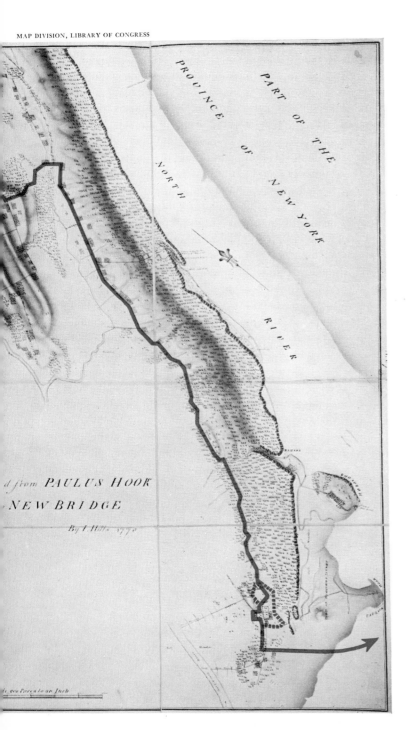

Part of "deserter" John Champe's route from the American camp to a British frigate lying off the Jersey shore opposite Manhattan (lower right) is here superimposed on a rare manuscript map of the area made by a British officer in 1770.

On the night of October 20, 1780, the weathered tents of the Continental Army were pitched in the rolling cattle country around Totowa above the Great Falls of the Passaic in New Jersey. Rain was making, and the night was moonless and black.

About ten o'clock, Sergeant Major John Champe of Lee's Light Horse Corps slipped past the camp guards and trotted out on the road that ran southeastward toward Bergen. Two British warships lay in Communipaw Bay, just beyond Bergen, and the deserting sergeant figured that with fair luck he would be safely aboard one of them by good daylight.

It was a full night's ride to the bay, and big John Champe settled to it. He was more than two miles on his way when a Continental outpost patrol came upon him from a side road. As the patrol halted and flung out a challenge, Champe spurred past and in a short race outran them. Furiously the patrol turned about and galloped for camp to report to the officer of the day that a deserter had managed to escape them.

A few minutes later, Captain Patrick Carnes stood before Major Henry Lee, asking permission to send off a pursuit party at once. Surprisingly, instead of agreeing to instant action, Lee reprimanded the captain severely for rousing him from sleep and professed to believe the whole report was exaggerated. He reminded Carnes that although desertions were common enough in the Continental Army, they were almost unheard of in his corps and ordered the captain to check the picket line for a missing horse. When Carnes returned and declared vehemently that not only was a horse missing but that he had discovered the deserter was Sergeant John Champe, Lee patronizingly told him he must be mistaken. Surely, said Lee, Champe had only gone off on an "excursion of pleasure," an offense grave enough, but not desertion.

If Captain Carnes was exasperated by the stub-

Strange Mission

f British-held New York

By GEORGE F. SCHEER

born incredulity of his major, he would have been astounded could he have known that Lee was deliberately delaying pursuit in order to help Champe get off safely to the enemy. For Champe's desertion had been intricately planned by Lee and the commander in chief, General Washington himself. While Lee temporized by preparing long written orders for the pursuit party, he alone knew that Champe was away upon the most bizarre secret mission of the Revolutionary War.

Less than a month before, the Continental Army had been stunned by the treachery of Benedict Arnold. Outwardly General Washington had taken Arnold's perfidy with the same cool reasonableness that usually marked his judgment. He had immediately sent two of his aides on a vain ride to intercept the fleeing traitor. He had reordered the positions of his army to protect the jeopardized fortress at West Point. Unhesitatingly he had endorsed the death sentence pronounced by a board of officers upon amiable and admired Major John André, Arnold's go-between, who had been unfortunate enough to fall into American hands.

But beneath his apparent calm, Washington was a man shaken and outraged. He desperately wanted Arnold—not merely to destroy him, but by a proper trial and sentence to make an example of him before his army and the world. But there was only one way to get him, and that was to snatch him bodily from the British Army in New York.

Washington talked it over with Henry Lee, and Lee, who had worked with the Continental espionage system and whose corps was full of men of enterprise, came up with the man for the job, Sergeant Major John Champe. Champe, a tall, muscular veteran of 23 or 24, had been singled out as a "very promising youth of uncommon taciturnity and inflexible perseverance." Lee, a fellow Virginian, also knew the Champe family of Loudoun County and was confident from both John Champe's "connections and his service in the army" that under every circumstance he would be "faithful" to his command.

Lee summoned Champe to his headquarters about nine o'clock the night of October 19, and after bolting the door behind him revealed to the dumfounded sergeant a daring plan: Champe was to desert to the British at New York. There he must manage to enlist in the corps that Benedict Arnold was known to be raising. He was to "insinuate himself" into a berth close to the traitor, while maintaining correspondence and meetings every second day with an American agent who would come in from Newark and make himself known as Mr. Baldwin. When a favorable night presented itself, they were somehow to seize Arnold and under cover of darkness get him across the Hudson to Bergen Woods, where an American patrol would meet them to escort them to headquarters. Mr. Baldwin would provide a boat on the appointed night.

To assure absolute secrecy, however, Champe must actually run every risk of any real deserter. The only aid Lee could promise him was to delay pursuit as long as possible after his desertion was discovered to give him a better chance to reach the enemy.

At first, Champe hesitated, not from fear but from repugnance at the idea of acting the deserter. Persuaded, however, by promise of a coveted promotion if he should succeed and the assurance that Lee would clear his name if he should meet with accident, he finally agreed to go after the traitor.

Lee immediately wrote to Washington, "I have engaged two persons to undertake the accomplishment of your Excellency's wishes. In my negotiation I have said little or nothing concerning your Excellency, as I presumed it would operate disagreeably should the issue prove disastrous." He had offered Champe promotion, he reported, and Mr. Baldwin, "one hundred guineas, five hundred acres of land, and three Negroes." If the scheme should fail, Mr. Baldwin still was to be paid the hundred guineas and "an additional sum of money."

"A few guineas," said Lee, "will be necessary" for Champe.

Washington promptly approved the plan as Lee out-

Benedict Arnold, the Target

lined it, "with this express stipulation and pointed injunction, that he, A——d, is brought to me alive. No circumstance whatever shall obtain my consent to his being put to death. The idea which would accompany such an event would be that ruffians had been hired to assassinate him. My aim is to make a public example of him."

The General sent five guineas for the sergeant, but shrewdly observed he was "not satisfied of the propriety of the sergeant's appearing with much specie. This circumstance may also lead to suspicion, as it is but too well known to the enemy that we do not abound in that article."

So on the night of the twentieth, Champe had conferred for the last time with Major Lee, packed his company orderly book and his personal belongings into his knapsack, and started his strange journey.

In all, Lee contrived to gain about an hour and a quarter's head start for Champe, before a squad of some fifteen dragoons thundered out of camp to chase him down. For hours Champe kept his lead, through Liberty Pole and the seven miles of forest called the English Neighbourhood to the vicinity of a popular tavern, the Three Pigeons, on the western slope of the ridge that flanked the salt marshes of the Hudson. But daylight caught him just emerging from the woods into the broad plain below the tavern. Suddenly the sound of horses came down to him on the sharp morning air. Glancing up he saw the dragoons on the eminence above the Three Pigeons.

Bergen was still four miles ahead. The village was the entry from the north to both the usual road to the British post at Paulus Hook and below it the road to Communipaw Bay. Champe guessed his pursuers would think he was bound for Paulus Hook and they would take a well-known short cut to the Paulus Hook

road to intercept him. When he reached the spot where the short cut forked left, he was momentarily hidden from the squad by a clump of woods. Instead of turning he roweled his mount and "at a venture" took the road straight to Bergen.

He had guessed well. His pursuers split into two parties to trap him at the bridge between Bergen and Paulus Hook, while he dashed through the village and sought the road running east a mile and a half to the bay. He had nearly reached the marshes on the shore when the squad, having discovered his deception and traced him through Bergen, came into sight again. He had just discarded his belt and scabbard, strapped his knapsack high on his shoulders, and plunged into the water when the dragoons enveloped his abandoned horse.

A British officer, observing the scene from the rail of one of the frigates, realized that an American deserter was trying to reach them and ordered a gun crew to cover him with grape shot, while a boat pushed off to pick him up. By a margin of fifty or sixty yards, and with the succor of the enemy, Champe was saved from the pistols of his own corps.

Aboard ship, Champe gave his name to his rescuers and said he wished to take British protection in New York. Very likely he was soon in the city, but it was Saturday, the twenty-first of October, and he was held until Monday for questioning.

The first hazardous step of the plot had been accomplished.

On Monday, October 23, 1780, in the beautiful high-ceilinged rooms of British Army Headquarters in the Kennedy mansion at 1 Broadway, John Champe was examined by Assistant Adjutant General George Beckwith. As the Continental sergeant told his story, Beckwith recorded it:

"October 23d. John Champe, Sergeant Major in Major Lee's Corps deserted from Passaic fall last Thursday night [it was Friday]. Major Lee's Corps consists of 90 mounted and one hundred dismounted. Marquis De Lafayette's infantry are there. Provisions very irregularly given out some days none. The Ration a pound fresh beef and ditto flour. The soldiery very much dissatisfied with the French."

Beckwith and the Brit-

FROM *Pictorial Field-Book of the Revo*

ish commander in chief, Sir Henry Clinton, found the "deserter's" story altogether acceptable. It added up. Many other malcontents had come over from the Continental Army with similar reports. The defection of a sergeant from a corps known even in the British Army for its staunch loyalty to the rebel cause, instead of arousing suspicion, on the contrary was taken as especially indicative of growing unrest among the Continentals.

Champe was offered the opportunity to enlist in the British Army, but he convinced his benefactors that to do so would too greatly increase his risk of being captured and hanged by the rebels, and they were satisfied to turn him loose to find employment in Manhattan. His next step was to place himself in the good graces of Benedict Arnold.

That task was simplified by the prominence and proximity of Arnold's quarters next door to Sir Henry's green-shuttered headquarters in the slightly less imposing but equally handsome dwelling at 3 Broadway. Almost within the hour after he left Beckwith, Champe "accidentally" ran into Arnold on the street. Still wearing his Light Horse uniform, it was easy enough to catch Arnold's eye and strike up conversation with the newly commissioned British Brigadier General. Champe's quiet, earnest manner seemed entirely convincing to Arnold as the Sergeant told him he had been inspired to desert a lost cause by Arnold's own example; the traitor offered him a post in his Loyalist Legion of similar rank to that which he had held in Lee's Corps. Accommodating the misgivings he had pretended to Clinton when offered a chance to enlist, Champe joined Arnold.

As a noncom in Arnold's Legion, Champe had easy access to the Colonel's quarters and person. No. 3 Broadway, looking out upon the now unkempt Bowling Green and across its trampled sod to the houses burned out in the 1776 fire, was almost at the very tip of the island. Beyond it to the south lay only Headquarters and imposing old Fort George and the Battery. The houses were almost flush with the sidewalk, but behind and north of 3 Broadway was a large

Major Henry Lee, the Planner

fenced garden which extended down to the black rocks of the Hudson's shore. North of the garden a seldom-used alley, also running out to the water's edge, separated the garden from the next property. Champe discovered that it was Arnold's unvarying habit to stroll in the garden each midnight before retiring; this was the place to seize him.

Over a period of days Champe worked loose three or four palings of the garden fence, so that under cover of dark he and his confederate could step noiselessly through them. He planned with Mr. Baldwin upon an appointed night to pounce on Arnold, stuff a gag in his mouth, and drag him through the fence into the alley. Holding him upright between them, they would drag him out of the alley, around the corner past 1 Broadway, and to a waiting boat at the pier behind the headquarters house. If the sentry at the doorstep of 1 Broadway challenged them, they would call out that they were taking a drunken companion home and hope to get off in the dark.

Establishing contact with Mr. Baldwin and through him keeping in touch with Lee had proved easy; by the twenty-fifth, two days after Champe had been examined at British Headquarters, Lee knew about the interrogation and about his fortuitous meeting with Arnold. But Champe was a cautious, deliberate sort, and he took his time perfecting the details of the kidnaping. It was December before he set a night, the eleventh, for taking Arnold. Lee was no longer in New Jersey. The Light Horse had gone south as an independent legion to join General Nathanael Greene's army in the Carolinas, and Champe was working with new contacts at Continental Army Headquarters.

During the tense afternoon hours of the eleventh, while Champe waited impatiently for the winter dark-

The kidnaping was to take place behind Arnold's Manhattan house, facing Bowling Green at 3 Broadway (second building from left). Just south was British Headquarters.

CONTINUED ON PAGE 100

This was the vast, empty, and often beautiful land through which Archbishop Lamy made his missionary rounds

CHURCHMAN *of the*

In the wild Southwest, Archbishop Lamy of Santa Fe contended with savag

He was spiritual leader of an area larger than his native France.

DESERT

Indians, ignorance, and a recalcitrant clergy

Winter storms in the Gulf of Mexico overtook a small ship beating her way from New Orleans to Galveston in January, 1851. Despite the fact that she had been condemned as unsafe, she carried 100 passengers. One of these was a French priest, 37 years old, who on November 24, 1850, in Cincinnati, Ohio, had been consecrated a bishop. Carrying with him the papal bull of Pius IX, which appointed him as vicar apostolic of New Mexico, he was on his way to Santa Fe. In the icy darkness of gales at sea he faced uncertainties, immediate and remote, for the ship held small promise of delivering him safely to shore, and he knew little enough of what might await him if he should survive the voyage.

In fact, he was traveling toward a job of work vast in scale. His new ecclesiastical province embraced a corner of present-day Nevada, about a fourth of Colorado, and all of Arizona and New Mexico except the southern strip which would presently be added by the Gadsden Purchase. Taken together, these lands were larger than the whole of his native France.

Their physical character was formidable—great elevated deserts divided at far intervals by forbidding mountains and threaded by only a few long, meager rivers with narrow belts of green life. There were few towns, and almost all of these lay widely separated along the valley of the Rio Grande in New Mexico. The population consisted largely of Spanish-Mexicans and Pueblo Indians. Until the year before they had belonged to the Mexican Republic; but in 1848 their territory had come to the United States as part of the settlement following the war with Mexico.

By PAUL HORGAN

Archbishop Lamy, about 1853

Previously, New Mexican ecclesiastical affairs had rested under the jurisdiction of the Bishop of Durango, in central Mexico, 1,500 miles from Santa Fe. When New Mexico and her adjacent areas became United States territory, not only civil affairs, but also the administration of the Church came within the new national frame. It was as a consequence of the Mexican War that social and religious conditions in the great Latin and Indian Southwest arrested the attention of the American bishops meeting in national council at Baltimore in the summer of 1849.

Periodically ever since 1630 the great lost province of Spain, and later of Mexico, on the northern Rio Grande, had asked for a bishop of its own to be seated at Santa Fe, but to no avail. Generations went by without an episcopal visitation to the exiled North, while mission friars struggled to hold their authority against the civil governors and even broke into quarrels with their distant and invisible bishop at Durango. In the early nineteenth century the long process of secularization began with the dismissal of the Franciscans, and without a bishop to guide it on the scene the Church fell upon unhappy days. The absence of a spiritual leader seemed like a symbol of the abandonment of the province. Who cared?—so far, so outlandish, with only a handful of Spaniards amidst a diffused population of Indians—New Mexico was lost in its golden distance, and the world did not appear to miss it.

Without leadership in the affairs of the spirit, the society lost any motive larger than that of simple survival. Ignorance was the heritage of each new generation. New Mexico had no schools. Her churches were for the most part in ruins. The Indian missions were abandoned. There were only nine priests in over 200,000 square miles. The deportment of some of these was at times reprehensible.

The state of affairs could hardly be worse, and one thing seemed clear to the council of bishops at Baltimore: so long as New Mexico's ecclesiastical responsibilities continued to come under the authority of the Bishop of Durango, her religious and social conditions could not be improved. The assembled bishops petitioned the Holy See to establish a vicariate apostolic for New Mexico, and to preside

Imported French artisans built Santa Fe's Cathedral of St. Francis. This water color is by Paul Horgan.

over it nominated Father Jean Baptiste Lamy, who had come to Kentucky from France in 1839 as a missionary priest. On July 19, 1850, Pope Pius IX approved the petition, and named as titular Bishop of Agathonica and vicar apostolic of New Mexico the man recommended to him.

When to his "great amazement and surprise" the papal bull with the news of his elevation reached Father Lamy in Kentucky he did not hesitate to accept, but in his heart he attached a condition, and his first act was to fulfill it by writing to his closest friend, Father Joseph P. Machebeuf, who was a pastor in Sandusky, Ohio.

"They wish," wrote Lamy of the Roman powers, "that I should be a Vicar Apostolic, and I wish you to be my Vicar General, and from these two vicars we shall try to make one good pastor. . . ."

These friends were born in the same department of France—Puy-de-Dôme in the Auvergne—and attended seminary together, and together came to America in 1839 when recruited as young missioners by Bishop Purcell of Cincinnati. Machebeuf consulted his superiors and his conscience. Both told him to go. He had to agree. With a sigh of regret for the faithful whom he was leaving, he yet kindled at the prospect of the adventure ahead.

Sharing a common dedication, the two vicars otherwise presented contrasts in appearance and personality. Lamy stood five feet ten inches in height, but his spare build made him seem taller. His manner was reposeful, but when he met people's gaze his dark eyes sparkled, and when he answered them his smile was persuasive. Patience, kindly gravity, and intelligence marked his face. All his life subject to spells of illness, he prevailed against them and went his way with his "usual and untiring energy." He was an expert horseman, with a good seat, erect in the saddle.

Machebeuf was of another type. He was a short man. His thin little frame seemed always to quiver with controlled animation. His hair was so light and his skin so pale that his classmates used to call him Whitey. His face was as plain as the Bishop's was handsome. Over his deep-set eyes he wore small spectacles with metal rims. Through all this there moved and reached a witty, compassionate and charming nature that raised people's spirits as they looked at him.

Nearing Galveston, Lamy's ship was driven aground in the shallows of the low coast. The Bishop lost most of his belongings, including "a fine new wagon which he bought at New Orleans for the trip over the plains," as Machebeuf later told. Lamy saw his trunk floating ashore in the wreckage, and with the help of a Negro boy salvaged it. It contained his vestments and his books, now waterlogged. The shipwreck cost him $350, a great sum for a new missionary bishop to lose.

He went on to San Antonio, where a United States Army train was making ready for a march to El Paso. He planned to go with it, and to carry Machebeuf and himself he bought a new buggy and a pair of newly broken mules. One day on a drive near San Antonio his coachman lashed the mules until they bolted. "I jumped out," said the Bishop, "and dislocated my ankle in the loose sand." He could not stand or walk. When Machebeuf arrived in San Antonio he found his friend laid up in pain. The army train had marched without him. It would be weeks until another went. Machebeuf brought him sad news—his sister had died in New Orleans. He needed all his fortitude to endure pain, loss, and idleness.

But presently they were on the way to the Rio Grande with another army train of 200 government wagons, 25 merchant wagons, a troop of cavalry, and stock animals. In six weeks they reached El Paso, where the pastor, a famous host, offered "every hospitality in his power." After years of never seeing a bishop, the El Paso priest now entertained his second within nine months, for in the preceding autumn Monsignor Zubiría, the Bishop of Durango, had paused at El Paso on his way to and from Santa Fe. The Mexican bishop's vast northern lands had already been transferred by the Holy See to an ecclesiastical jurisdiction within the United States—but he did not know it then, and the pastor of El Paso could not say if he knew it even now.

In this confusion lay the seed of heavy trouble for the new bishop. For when, after a progress northward through the Rio Grande towns, where he passed beneath triumphal arches of evergreens erected by jubilant villagers, he came to his capital on August 8, 1851, he found the local clergy respectful of his purple, but otherwise waiting to greet him with discouraging news. Receiving a great civic welcome at Santa Fe, the vicar apostolic was informed by Father Ortíz, the vicar in Santa Fe of the Bishop of Durango, that he and his clergy must refuse to accept him as their new superior.

But the papal bull, the letters of appointment? Bishop Lamy displayed them.

They might be in order, to be sure; but Father Ortíz had received from Durango no word of any change of administration; and until he had this he could not resign his powers to Bishop Lamy, and his priests must not consider themselves subject to a new lordship.

Lamy considered the matter from the local point of view and patiently concluded that in official terms the vicar of Santa Fe was justified in his position. There was only one thing to do. The vicar apostolic must go, himself, on a longer and harder journey than the one he had just made. It would take him to the city of Durango, where he would have to present his case to old Bishop Zubiría and convince him that it was just.

Delegating Father Machebeuf to act for him in his absence and giving orders that a school for the teaching of English be established at Santa Fe without delay, he rode out on a mule in late September for the episcopal city 1,500 miles away. With him he took only a guide—and Vicar Ortíz.

In Santa Fe Machebeuf saw a one-story town built of adobes—earthen bricks plastered over with more earth. Threading away from the long central plaza, the principal streets, about a mile long, were irregularly parallel to the Santa Fe Creek. Five or six thousand people lived in the capital. Trade was lively. Gambling, drinking, and dancing, in both American and Mexican styles, animated the public airs of evening. The city lay at 7,000 feet of altitude under changeable glories of sky and mountain light. Its social character was little modified since its foundation in 1610.

"This is a country of ancient Catholicity," wrote Machebeuf in his first impressions. "The people in general show the best disposition. . . . But alas! the great obstacle to the good which the Bishop is disposed to do among them, does not come from the people but from the priests themselves, who do not want the bishop, for they dread reform in their morals, or a change in the selfish relations with their parishioners. One of the great neglects of the priests of New Mexico is that they seldom or never preach." Then, having seen how they lived, Machebeuf added in wrath, "But how could such priests preach?"

The Bishop was home in time for Christmas. He had much to tell his great friend. Bishop Zubiría had renounced any claim to New Mexico. He examined Lamy's papal bull, and at once said, "I knew nothing about it officially." Under the circumstances, how could he, or his clergy in turn, have submitted to another prelate? But "this document is sufficient authority for me," he said with grace, "and I submit to it." Monsignor Zubiría ordered the preparation of papers in which he renounced his jurisdiction over the vast northern province.

Promptly upon Lamy's return, Zubiría's instrument of renunciation was posted for all to see. Any of the clergy who refused to accept it, and any who did not mend their ways, were released from their duties, to depart from New Mexico. To those who remained the new bishop and his vicar general served as examples. It was time to go to work.

Most of the native priests responded with obedience, but in a few cases the Bishop was forced to resort to severe measures. The pastors of Albuquerque, Taos, and Arroyo Hondo defied him in various degrees of disobedience. When after repeated warnings they persisted in their defiance, the Bishop acted to suspend them from priestly functions and even in two cases, to excommunicate them. Father Machebeuf was sent in each instance to execute the Bishop's sentence.

The recusant pastors had their partisans, and in Taos, particularly, followers of Father José Antonio Martínez threatened an outbreak like the Taos Rebellion of 1847 with its bloodshed. But Machebeuf, too, had powerful friends in Taos, one of whom was Kit Carson. "I am a man of peace," said Carson, "and my motto is: good will to all; I hate disturbances among the people, but I can fight a little yet, and I know of no better cause to fight for than my family, my church, and my friend the Señor Vicario."

When the vicar general came to do his duty his friends saw to it that armed men were stationed about the village to defend him and his mission. He accomplished it from the altar of Taos in a scene of great tenseness, and a week later repeated it at Arroyo Hondo. Peace held. The Bishop never again was forced to show what such cases of discipline showed—that the clergy must be worthy of their vocations, and that there was strength in the new administration of the Church in New Mexico.

To fulfill his vision of his duty, the young bishop had to proceed from the abstraction of a map to the reality of his people and their far separated places on the great open land. He crossed desert and mountain, traveling tens of thousands of miles on mule or horse, making the hard country yield up to him its blind ways. Machebeuf, too, often went into the country as a simple missioner. Between them they tried to rectify the neglect of centuries. When new friends whom he traveled to serve asked where he lived, Machebeuf would reply: "In the saddle . . . they call me El Vicario Andando, the Traveling Vicar, and I live on the public highway." Lamy could say the same. His duties sent him east and west by wagon several times on the Santa Fe Trail.

In contrast to the elaborate cathedral in Santa Fe, which Lamy commissioned, are the simple adobe churches of rural New Mexico. One of them, the former Spanish mission at Taos, is shown here. Starkly handsome, it glows in the golden light of a desert sunset.

In 1852 Lamy's wagon overtook a larger train of 25 others bound for New Mexico with merchandise from Saint Louis for the five Spiegelberg brothers, whom he had already come to know in Santa Fe where their famous emporium on the plaza did a thriving business. As the Bishop approached he saw that the wagon train was halted. Someone from the train was being carried by Mexican teamsters into an abandoned sod hut. It was Levi Spiegelberg, they explained, and they were sure he had cholera. Out of fear they refused to travel with him.

The Bishop went to Levi without hesitation and said to him, "Good friend, we willingly make room for you in our covered wagon and will nurse you until you regain your strength, for we could not think of leaving you here in this lonely prairie cabin. We do not believe you have cholera, and even if you have we are not afraid of contagion." The Bishop and the priests who accompanied him took care of the sick man, who was cured in a week.

Two months later when they all arrived in Santa Fe, the story was told to the other Spiegelberg brothers—handsome and cultivated men—and ever afterward the whole family and the Bishop were devoted friends. On a later prairie voyage—in 1867—cholera actually did strike the Bishop's train, and two of his party died, including a young American nun. During her illness,

ANSEL ADAMS FROM *Arizona Highways,* COURTESY *Life*

the train was attacked at the Arkansas River crossing by 300 Comanche Indians. For three hours they continued their attack, circling in single file about the parked wagons and keeping up a steady fire. Among the wagoners who fought back was the Bishop, who handled a musket.

For his duties required him to excel in the frontiersman's craft, and many a night going alone on missionary journeys he slept "under the moon," as he said, and sometimes he crossed as many as 75 miles without water, and often he walked in order to rest his horse. The prairies he called "beautiful and vast." His first venture into Arizona covered 3,000 miles and lasted six months and he said his Christmas Mass there on a snow-covered slope of a mountain forest. After his long pastoral journeys to Colorado, he told of its cold heights, its great rivers pounding out of the mountains into wide valleys, like the San Luis, where in his

CONTINUED ON PAGE 99

35

Nathan Meeker

Even when death struck suddenly,

the starry-eyed Indian agent was

still dreaming of turning his

Ute wards into white men overnight

Arvilla Delight Meeker

THE BLOODY END OF

MEEKER'S UTOPIA

By MARSHALL SPRAGUE

On September 29, 1879, a small band of Ute Indians went wild on the Western Slope of Colorado and murdered their Indian agent and all his employees at the remote Ute Agency on White River. A few hours earlier, another small Ute band ambushed a relief force of soldiers at Milk Creek 25 miles away. All told, the White River Utes, who had never hurt anybody before, killed 30 white men and wounded 44 more.

The murdered agent, Nathan Meeker, did not resemble the average second-rater sent out by the Indian Office as a political favor. Meeker was a newspaper editor and a writer of wide repute, and his violent death in the romantic Rocky Mountain wilderness shocked and thrilled the whole nation. In addition, the White River massacre gave Coloradans the pretext they had sought for a decade to take from the Utes their vast hunting paradise of 12,000,000 acres.

The hideous climax of Meeker's career derived from starry-eyed idealism, which he had cultivated all his life. He was born in 1817 on a breezy Ohio homestead overlooking Lake Erie. At seventeen he ran away from home to become a poet, starved a while as a young intellectual on MacDougal Street in New York and returned prosaically to Ohio to run a general store. He married a sea captain's gray-eyed daughter, Arvilla Delight Smith, who bore him three daughters and two

sons. She was a plain, pious girl, always a little embarrassed about her fecundity and apprehensive about her husband who theorized brilliantly but disliked manual labor and talked of Jesus Christ as though He were a fairly sound but not entirely respectable neighbor down the street.

Meeker was often broke and twice bankrupt during the first twenty nomadic years of their marriage. In Ohio, and later in Illinois, Arvilla and the children often tended his store while he dabbled in Fourier socialism, Phalangist economics, planned parenthood, Brook Farm Transcendentalism, a Buddhist sort of Christianity, and the practice of nibbling carrots for better vision at night.

His yearning to improve the world expressed itself at last in his first novel, *The Adventures of Captain Armstrong*, the hero of which was tall, handsome, coolheaded, plausible, and indestructibly hopeful like himself. The captain was shipwrecked on a Polynesian atoll and in jig time created among the naked savages a co-operative Utopia of modern industries and crafts. Meeker was a great admirer of Horace Greeley, the famous editor of the New York *Tribune*. He mailed his novel to Greeley, who found a publisher for it. Later, Greeley made Meeker his war correspondent to cover for the *Tribune* Grant's Mississippi campaign.

Then he brought him to New York to be his agricultural editor.

Meeker was a persuasive columnist and he became a national oracle on farm problems. But in 1869 his Utopian dreams crystallized in a plan for a co-operative farm colony near Denver in semi-arid Colorado Territory. Horace Greeley approved the plan and gave him free space in the *Tribune* to promote it. Members of this Union Colony (Meeker called his new town "Greeley") had to be temperate, industrious, moral, and tolerant in their religious outlook.

The founder visited the Cache la Poudre region northeast of Denver and chose a flat, wind-swept tract which was to become the most successful co-operative venture in the Rockies. The tract, like the rest of the Great Plains, had no rainfall to speak of. Meeker's colonists watered their new farms by an elaborate system of ditches which distributed the snow water flowing down from the mountains seventy miles away. Their irrigation methods were copied widely. Their success made it possible to grow crops and livestock in quantity on small acreages. Colorado villages began expanding into cities, the mining districts swarmed with new people, and homesteaders poured into Colo-

rado Territory, enabling it to win statehood in 1876.

Meanwhile the fates conspired to destroy Meeker. He was not a good executor of his own theories (his first irrigation ditch at Greeley cost Union Colony $25,000 and watered less than 200 acres, including the basements of several business establishments). He frittered away his small capital on his Utopia and on his newspaper, the Greeley *Tribune*. He went deeply in debt to Horace Greeley, himself, before the great editor died in 1872. By degrees, his colonists watered down his idealistic aims and eased him out of power. As his frustrations accumulated, he grew brusque and opinionated. He denounced traveling theatricals and dancing and picking wildflowers. He blackballed from membership in the Greeley Farmers' Club all those who opposed his views.

In 1877 the executors of Horace Greeley's estate demanded the money which he owed to it. Desperately

All was peaceful for the Utes when this picture was taken in Washington about 1874. Chief Ouray is second from right, front row; Jack and Johnson, later massacre leaders, are second and third from right, back row. Among their white friends is Otto Mears (right), the fabulous western capitalist.

Meeker sought and failed to get a postmastership. He applied for but was not accepted for duty at the Paris Exposition. Then he heard that an Indian agent was needed at the White River Ute Agency in northwest Colorado. He had no special interest in Indians as yet, but the job paid $1,500 a year. To get it, he sought the aid of old newspaper friends back East and some influential Coloradans like Senator Teller. Because of their recommendations, Carl Schurz, secretary of the interior under President Hayes, assigned him to the White River Ute Agency.

The assignment transformed the harried Utopian. He was only 61, but the bitter disappointments at Greeley had given him a defeated look. He had grown thin and stooped, as though bent by the burden of his own despair. As hope returned, his imagination resumed its extravagant soaring. His blue eyes sparkled. His stoop vanished. His shoulders swung confidently when he walked, like the swinging, confident shoulders of his fictional superman, Captain Armstrong.

As he applied his idealism to the problems of the Utes, he began telling himself that maybe he wasn't through yet. Maybe he could achieve Captain Arm-strong's Utopia after all. And perhaps, after he had taught the wonders of modern society to these simple White River savages, a grateful President Hayes might ask him to perform the same miracle for the Sioux and Apaches and all the other suffering red men!

Leaving the Greeley *Tribune* in the hands of a friend, Meeker set out for his new post early in May, 1878. Arvilla and his youngest daughter Josie were to follow him there in mid-summer. The other two girls agreed to run the family home as a boarding house. The new Indian agent was hardly aware of the explosive situation into which he stepped during his five-day trek to White River. The seeds of bitter conflict over possession of Colorado's Western Slope had been a long time sprouting. The Colorado Utes, anciently of Aztec breeding, had endured centuries of misery as pariahs until the seventeenth century, when they became among the first, if not the very first, Indians to adopt the horse from Spanish colonists on the Rio Grande. This magical creature so inspired them as to completely change their tribal personality. They developed into superb horsemen and found themselves able to hold the Colorado highlands for their exclu-

NEW YORK *Illustrated Times,* FROM CULVER SERVICE

Eastern tabloids reported the White River massacre with considerable license, as this draw-ing indicates. That Josie Meeker wielded a rifle against the attackers is pure fantasy.

sive use. Thereafter their reverence was boundless for the divine beast which had raised them from the depths of human degradation to great happiness, prosperity, and dignity.

Eventually some 3,500 of these Utes divided into six loosely allied Colorado bands, led by an extraordinary man named Chief Ouray. He was 45 in 1878 and had a mind as spacious as his mountains. He had risen to power in 1863 and had set his political policy then. The Utes, he decreed, must live in peace with white men. They must modify their wasteful hunting economy, sell off bits of land as required by events, and learn to prosper on the reduced acreage as white men prospered.

Ouray's masterpiece was the Treaty of 1868 by which the U.S. Senate gave his six bands most of Colorado's Western Slope forever (4,500 acres for each Ute man, woman, and child). In 1873 he had to release the 4,000,000-acre San Juan silver region but the Utes had a 12,000,000-acre reservation left. They were still the richest Indian landed gentry in the nation. And they were the pets of the whites, befriending settlers and doing a big buckskin business with traders.

But Ouray played a losing game. By 1878 the tenfold increase in the state's white population had created a huge demand for more land. Politically, the demand was expressed in an outcry for the removal of the Colorado Utes and the liquidation of their vast Western Slope estate. Senator Teller and the land grabbers around him dreamed of herding them off to army-guarded desert camps. But the Teller crowd had to move with caution because of the good reputation of Ouray's people. Their strategy was to try to destroy this reputation by accusing the Utes falsely of all kinds of outrage, arson, theft, and murder.

The Utes were deeply disturbed by the charges, the resentment being highest among the two White River bands under the aging Chief Douglas and Chief Jack. This Jack was a young, forceful leader and he reacted to the white campaign of slander by urging an end to Ouray's peace policy. He wanted the Utes to fight for their homeland, though Ouray warned him that he was playing into Senator Teller's hands. Ouray added that if the Utes went on the warpath, they would abrogate their treaty rights and lose all they possessed.

Chief Jack was not convinced. The government, he said, had always mistaken Ouray's peace policy for weakness and was preparing to dispossess the Utes anyway. He stressed that Interior Secretary Schurz had just dismissed the White River agent who had protected their rights for years. Schurz had replaced this good agent with a Teller appointee named Nathan Meeker. In Jack's opinion, such an appointee could

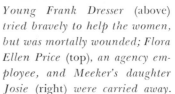

Young Frank Dresser (above) *tried bravely to help the women, but was mortally wounded; Flora Ellen Price* (top), *an agency employee, and Meeker's daughter Josie* (right) *were carried away.*

have but two aims; to steal Ute land and destroy the Ute way of life.

On May 10, 1878, the new agent arrived blithesomely at the cluster of tumble-down log buildings in White River valley at the utter end of the 185-mile road south from Rawlins, Wyoming. The bleak agency setting did not resemble Captain Armstrong's charming atoll in the South Seas, but Meeker did not care. He was abloom with love for and faith in his Utes and had high hopes of easing their presumed misery. He was not worried about the hostility which greeted him at first. He placated many Indians soon by his success in obtaining better rations and distributing annuities on time. They were pleased too with his agency staff—eight good-natured young men hand-picked by Meeker from the best families in Greeley.

The agent outlined his Utopian dream to the principal chiefs, Douglas and Jack, and to the head medicine man, Johnson, a distinguished horseman who was also Ouray's brother-in-law. Meeker explained how he would teach them modern farming and irrigation so that they could all be rich, live in houses, ride in carriages, use privies, sleep in beds, wear underwear, and send their children to the agency school. He described plans for associated industries to raise their living standard still higher—saw mills, orchards, wool plants, coal mines, and a railroad to Rawlins.

He observed that Douglas and Johnson were mildly intrigued by his dream. But Jack had an irritating way of asking loaded questions. He asked whether or not white men would allow Utes to compete in business with them. He wanted to know if the high living standard of the whites was worth all the work and

CONTINUED ON PAGE 90

When Everything Hung by a Thread

The business boom in the post-Civil War decades spawned an arresting advertising device fully as charming as it was effective— the trade or premium card. Given away by merchants, usually to the children of customers, they were welcomed into the American home for their bright lithographed color and their depictions of the newest developments in an age of rapid change. Many families even saved their favorites in scrapbooks. These thread industry cards are from the collection of Samuel Rosenberg.

This 1880's card noted that Bartholdi's masterpiece was soon to grace New York Harbor, but on the back of it cautioned that the base and torch shown were "purely allegorical."

The ingenious thread people invoked popular symbols to put their message across. The somewhat dudish cowboy (above) was evidently meant to recall the exploits of Buffalo Bill, while Swift's character (right) was immediately familiar to young and old. Such advertising techniques were successful enough to keep some 200 lithographers busy turning out cards during the peak years.

Leading lights of the day were fair game for advertisers. The card at left is a jibe at Oscar Wilde, who had recently arrived for his American tour carrying a posy.

On the card below a visiting French celebrity, Jean François Gravelet, known to his admirers as the great Blondin, is shown negotiating his tightrope of thread.

JUMBO MUST GO, BECAUSE DRAWN BY WILLIMANTIC THREAD!

The trade card designers vaunted the tensile strength of thread by using such popular marvels as Barnum's huge pachyderm, Jumbo.

Belding Brothers linked their product to the latest thing in transportation. Spools of thread run the mechanism of the cable car shown at right.

41

First by Land

The river that disappointed him bears his name, but Alexander Mackenzie's

great achievement in slogging to the Pacific is now almost forgotten

By MORTON M. HUNT

The most momentous event in the geographical history of the North American continent, aside from its discovery, was the first complete crossing of it from coast to coast—a feat that was three centuries in the doing. This epochal achievement first confirmed the guesses of civilized man about the breadth and structure of the continent and led directly to the opening up of the West. Yet millions of Americans—indeed, most of us—know neither the date it was done nor the name of the man who did it.

Contrary to popular belief, it was neither Lewis nor Clark. Eleven years before they set out on their famous expedition—when Clark was still a young lieutenant fighting Indians on the Ohio River frontier and Lewis was a teen-age youth in Virginia—the man who would first conquer the continent was already on the last lap of his trip, paddling up an unknown river in western Canada two thousand miles beyond the frontiers of civilization.

He was Alexander Mackenzie, a thirty-year-old Scotsman in the fur trade. Mackenzie was attempting to breach the fabled Rockies, thread his way through the unknown rivers, chasms, and forests of the West, and slip unharmed through more than six hundred miles of savage-infested wilderness. He expected to accomplish this with a total expeditionary force of nine canoemen and himself, equipped with several rifles, one birchbark canoe, and three thousand pounds of food, clothing, and trading gifts. Mackenzie was one of that long-vanished breed of explorers who need

nothing of civilized man's benefits except his spirit.

Civilized man himself was, in that year 1793, established firmly only along the Atlantic coast and up the river valleys of the East. He knew little of the vast central plains, and the soaring uplands of the West were a white blank on his maps. But one leathery, hard-bitten type had explored many hundreds of miles beyond the comfortable houses and streets of Montreal and Detroit. This was the fur trader, who dared to live among the Indians and barter for the pelts that Europe was so eager to buy.

The men of the North-West Company (the major competitor of the Hudson's Bay Company) had learned to travel in Indian fashion, and so had been able without roads, wagons, or horses to push deep into the continent. Via the St. Lawrence River and the Great Lakes, and thence by canoe through a tangled network of rivers, lakes, and forest portages, they gradually probed into the primeval wilderness of central Canada. In this great unknown they built a slender chain of tiny forts, which, by 1793, lay strung three-quarters of the way across the continent.

Alexander Mackenzie was one of these men. Born in Scotland, he came to America as a youth to make his fortune and worked for five years at a fur trader's

A young chief guided Mackenzie and his men to the mouth of the treacherous Bella Coola River. They made their final dash to the Pacific in a canoe borrowed from the Indians, as shown in this romantic painting by Frederic Remington.

accounting desk in Montreal. Then he broke away from the countinghouse and went into the back country; here he toughened his body and mastered the skills of the explorer and fur trader. Soon he began pushing beyond the boundaries of the known trading area, trying to find new tribes and new river routes to the untapped regions.

Such exploring meant sleeping on the ground in freezing weather, living in filthy buckskins for months at a time, suffering the torments of fleas and mosquitoes, and enduring an almost suffocating loneliness with only illiterate Indians and French-Canadian *voyageurs* for companionship.

Mackenzie, as he looked when knighted in 1802.

journeyed again to the trading regions, moving on from fort to fort, and finally pushing hundreds of miles beyond the last of them to build himself a new outpost in which to pass the winter.

Fork Fort, as he called it, was nothing more than a cluster of small log cabins surrounded by a palisade fence. It lay on a bank of the Peace River near the fork of the Smoky in what is now northern Alberta, several hundred miles north of the present United States-Canadian border and about as far west as modern Boise, Idaho; near that site today stands the little town of Peace River. This was as far as he could go before the winter of

Mackenzie himself later referred, in his laconic Scottish manner, to "the many tedious and weary days, the gloomy and inclement nights, and the toilsome exertions" of his explorations.

Ostensibly, profit was his motive; a man could become rich in a decade of fur trading if he survived it and if he kept bringing in the pelts. But there was more to it than potential profit. For, once the idea had seized him of being the first man to complete the crossing of the continent, it would not let him go. He gradually and hopelessly fell in love with it, as men in all ages have fallen in love with the idea of discovering something still unknown to the rest of mankind.

In 1789 Mackenzie finally launched himself and a small party of canoemen on a broad river that flowed west from Great Slave Lake, hoping it would carry him to the Pacific. He knew little of navigation, and when the river veered northward, he was unable to reckon how far off course he was going. Fifteen hundred miles later, he and his men found themselves canoeing along the shores of the Arctic Ocean, with the huge bulk of Alaska still between them and the Pacific.

Bitterly disappointed, he returned to his trading post in central Canada, but the dream would not leave him in peace. In 1791 he made the long, hard trip back to Montreal and thence to London, where he privately studied astronomy and navigation until he felt ready; the next year he came back to Canada and

1792-93 set in and froze his river routes. In the spring he readied his supplies, and on May 9, 1793, he and nine men—one Scotsman, six French-Canadians, and two Indian hunters—pushed off to conquer the Rocky Mountains in a canoe.

You might suppose that a man who could undertake such an adventure must have been ice-cold, steel-hard, and utterly fearless. Such indeed was the thin-lipped, gray-eyed young man as his canoemen saw him; but secretly he was tormented, torn by doubts and fears, and unsure of his own abilities. "I am so vexed and disturbed of late," he wrote before the start of the journey, "that I cannot sit down to anything steadily." If his timorous men had known it, the trip might never have gotten started, but Mackenzie was able to mask his feelings behind a calm, impassive face.

At first the trip went smoothly. Each morning Mackenzie woke his men at about 3 A.M. Among *voyageurs* it was the custom then to order a dram of rum all around, then in a matter of minutes roll the blankets up and be off in the canoe, puffing clay pipes and sometimes chanting a canoeman's ballad for several hours of hard paddling before breakfast. With a few brief pauses, Mackenzie's men continued on all day until 7 P.M., when they stopped, cooked dinner, pitched the tent, and then rolled themselves in their blankets and fell asleep on the hard ground. For eight days they proceeded in this fashion up the Peace River into the foothills of the Rockies, through a succession of green meadows and rolling hills; then, at 2 P.M. on May 17, they could for the first time see in the distance the faint snow-capped peaks of the Rockies. Soon afterward their troubles began.

As they approached the mountains, the river grew narrower and swifter, and the banks on either side became steep, rising sheer and rocky. By the nineteenth of May they were deep into the Peace River Canyon, an almost 25-mile-long zigzag slash in the backbone of the mountain range. Instead of smoothly paddling upstream as they had for the first eight days, now they had to fight for every yard against the rushing water, with the fragile canoe creaking and lurching under them. Their goods got soaked, had to be unpacked and dried in the sun, were repacked, and got soaked again.

So the day went—towing, poling, paddling, repairing rips in the canoe with spruce fibers and pine gum, unpacking to portage around impassable places, escaping from one near-disaster only to face another, until the sun went down and the chill wind bit into their fingers. "I could not but reflect, with infinite anxiety, on the hazard of my enterprize," Mackenzie later admitted; but he concealed his anxiety behind a front of crisp command and constant reassurance to his exhausted and frightened men.

The next day was even worse. In one two-mile stretch they had to unload, portage, and reload four times, and finally they reached a spot from which they could see nothing ahead but unbroken rapids. There was a narrow beach of broken rock fragments just wide enough to permit them to tow the bouncing canoe along while the bowman and steersman stayed aboard and fought to keep her from being smashed against the rocks. Yard by yard, step by step, they worked their way upstream. Then suddenly one extra-violent wave broke over the bow and snapped the strained towline with a sickening twang.

For an endless instant Mackenzie watched, horrified, as his only means of transportation and the men in the boat were swept backwards toward destruction. But in the next second another freakish wave swept the canoe up and over a line of jagged rocks and washed her, unscratched, within a few feet of the bank. The canoemen instantly beached her and tumbled onto land, where the others joined them, shaken, white-faced, and muttering rebelliously.

Several men spoke out plainly, saying that it was impossible to proceed; the Indians had all told them so long ago; they would go no further. Mackenzie ignored all this and brusquely ordered the most outspoken of the men to get busy and find a way up the side of the canyon in order to locate a suitable camp site for the night. He summoned one of his two Indians to follow

him and went off at once to reconnoiter. Behind him the *voyageurs*, their mood of rebellion nipped short, sullenly got to work.

The canyon ahead, as Mackenzie learned after a two-hour trip, was absolutely impassable, and its banks were too steep for portaging. He could think of no alternative except to carry the 25-foot canoe and its ton and a half of goods up and over the densely forested mountain, rejoining the river on the other side of it where presumably the canyon would end. It was, as he noted in his daily logbook, an "alarming" prospect; but a day of rest and preparation, and a hot meal of wild rice and sugar with the "usual regale" of rum on the side, gave his men courage enough to try it.

At daybreak on the twenty-second they began one of the most outlandish jobs of portaging in the annals of exploration. At the foot of the steep slope they began felling trees with their axes, dropping them parallel to the path and not completely severed from the stumps, as per Mackenzie's orders, so as to make a crude railing on either side. As soon as a sizeable part of the pathway had been cleared, Mackenzie put several men onto the job of bringing up the supplies.

Bit by bit they brought everything up from the river as far as the camp site, and then went back for the canoe. This they had to hoist up the cliff a yard or so at a time, one man keeping a taut bowline about a tree above while the others heaved and lifted from below. Beyond the camp site they used the same method till they reached the summit of the steep slope.

The next day the ascent became less rugged as they got beyond the canyon walls. The men continued to work in two groups, one going ahead and chopping out a path through the woods, the other bringing up the goods and the canoe. The ground was a succession of hills and defiles, and the woods gave way to thorny briar and dense underbrush which were terrible to clear away. Sometimes it must have seemed madness to go another yard. "At five," Mackenzie later recalled, "in a state of fatigue that may be more readily conceived than expressed, we encamped near a rivulet." They had made three miles that day.

The third day of the mountain portage went a little better, as they began to work their way down the steep slopes. By four that afternoon they had come four more miles; shaking with weariness, they suddenly emerged from a dense stand of pine and saw the river before them, calm, wide, and placid. A little way downstream it narrowed, plunged between vertical rocks, and then broke into foaming rapids. The mountain portage, about eight miles long in all, had brought them out just above the beginning of the Peace River Canyon and had pierced the first great ridge of mountains leading them into the heart of the Rockies.

Now the river wound around crookedly in an elevated area cradled by the Rocky Mountains on all sides. For six uneventful days they paddled steadily upstream, seeing signs of Indians, but meeting none. On May 31 they arrived at a fork where two rivers joined, one coming from the northwest and the other from the southeast; the former seemed to be in the right direction and was broad and calm, while the latter seemed to lie in the wrong direction and was narrow and swift.

The men argued vehemently for the former, and Mackenzie himself would have preferred it; but he believed in the wisdom of the Indians, and he was determined to follow the route an old Beaver Indian warrior had described to him months ago. He ordered his paddlers to take the southeast fork. (He was wise to follow the Indian's advice; this fork was the Parsnip River, which was to prove a useful route; the other, now called the Finlay, would have merely lost him among steeper mountains to the north.)

In the following days Mackenzie knew many hours of discouragement and despair. The Parsnip, now at flood, was a difficult river for canoemen, so swift that any progress was exhausting. The canoe ripped open, but they patched and regummed it. Only Mackenzie's continually varied techniques of handling his men kept them on their way; as for him, the hope of finding a portage to a west-flowing river which he could follow downstream to the Pacific seemed to fade day by day.

For already he had come nearly 400 roundabout miles and used up one month of the precious, short-lived summer; if he did not soon find the legendary portage of which the old Indian had spoken, all would be in vain. Then on the afternoon of June 9 he smelled smoke and heard the sound of people rushing about in the woods just ahead. They turned out to be a little band of rather scraggly Indians who shouted defiantly and made warlike gestures; but Mackenzie, who was sympathetic to the Indian mind, recognized that they were more frightened than bellicose. Patiently and gently he made overtures through his two Indian hunters, and after some two hours of reassurances the Indians and the explorers were assembled amiably about a campfire, exchanging gifts and information.

They told Mackenzie that they knew of no down-flowing river which emptied into the "Stinking Lake" (the Indians' name for the Pacific). The impatient explorer questioned the Indians for hours, passed a sleepless night, and was up at dawn to resume his interrogation. "The Sun, however," he related, "had risen before they left their leafy bowers, whither they had retired with their children, having most hospitably resigned their beds, and the partners of them, to the solicitations of my young men." Finally he learned that one of them did know of a west-flowing river, but it did *not* empty into the ocean. He was greatly relieved; he supposed that the native had never followed the river to the Pacific and therefore simply did not understand that it had to empty there.

Having persuaded one of the Indians to accompany the party as a guide, Mackenzie pushed off again. For two days they worked their way up ever-narrower and shallower streams until they reached a tiny lake which was the source of the Parsnip-Peace system. Here they found a beaten path, apparently a much-used portage, and carried their goods and their canoe along it. As they passed over a low ridge, Mackenzie saw several rivulets tumbling down some nearby rocks; two of the streams flowed back to the east, and two others flowed on toward the west. "We are now going with the stream," he noted confidently.

But the first week of the descent was frightfully difficult. They were wrecked once in a boiling rapids and later had to cut a portage through forest and swamp for three days. Finally they arrived at a wide navigable river (later named the Fraser) which flowed southerly before winding toward the Pacific. Down this river they proceeded with relative ease, gaining more mileage in three days than they had in the previous seven or eight.

Thus far there had been many a situation where only Mackenzie's courage—vastly greater than that of the tough, forest-hardened men under him—had pulled the expedition through; now came an even more remarkable example of that cold, perfect self-control which he was so often able to assume at will. On their fourth day along the Fraser, a large group of Indian warriors swarmed out onto the river bank, shouting fiercely and loosing a volley of arrows that dropped all around the canoe.

Mackenzie wanted desperately to talk to them about the river route ahead, but no words of his Indian hunters could pacify the wild mob. Finally, relying on his own insight into Indian psychology, he decided on a daring approach. Beaching his canoe on the opposite shore, he ordered his men to remain in sight of the hostile warriors, while he himself walked alone far up the bank.

As he expected, two of the braves now came over in a canoe, curious and eager to inspect him, yet still more frightened than bloodthirsty. With soft words, friendly gestures, and the offer of mirrors and some beads, he soon made friends with them and sent them back to their tribe to carry the word. In a short time the explorers and the Carrier Indians (as they were later called by white men) were gathered together, jabbering away at each other without hostility.

At first adverse reports of the river beyond did not deter Mackenzie; but as he continued downstream they were repeated with a discouraging frequency. The Carrier Indians told him that the Fraser not only became wild and impassable, but that warlike tribes would certainly annihilate his little band. In any event, the river was said to be very long and roundabout and altogether too slow a route for Mackenzie's diminished supplies.

Mackenzie was dreadfully downcast, thinking of the wasted effort and the impossibility of continuing downstream. As often happened, he betook himself to one side to mull in solitude. But soon, as he later told the story, "instead of continuing to indulge [these reflections], I determined to proceed with resolution, and set future events at defiance." Knowing from coastal exploration data where the Pacific lay, and knowing his own present position, he calculated there were about 200 miles remaining and decided to strike off overland and *walk* toward the Pacific. If this seemed a wild scheme, it was at least better than giving up altogether.

But what would be the point of such an endeavor, even if it succeeded? He had started out to find a fur-trade route to the Pacific, but a route that involved a two-week walk would be totally impractical. In that sense, his exploration was already a failure.

Yet Mackenzie had long since lost his purely monetary motives and now was being driven on by the desire for pure knowledge. Alexander Mackenzie, a bewhiskered, hard-working mercantile adventurer, was thoroughly under the sway of that most civilized quality we call "intellectual curiosity."

Before quitting the river, Mackenzie spent several days having his men build a complete new canoe from fresh bark and cached it and some food for their return. On July 4 they finally struck off on foot with an Indian guide. Their departure point was just above the Blackwater River, a small branch of the Fraser which lies in the central part of British Columbia.

For the next two weeks they struggled westward, laboring up and down the mountain slopes with ninety-pound packs of food and gear on their backs. Gradually the portage eased as they descended from the semibarren uplands into the luxuriant forests of the Pacific coastal slope. A young brave would guide them from his tribe's village to that of the next tribe, where he would introduce them, get from Mackenzie a knife or piece of cloth in payment, and then return home. Mackenzie would meanwhile dicker for a new

CONTINUED ON PAGE 94

This map of western Canada shows routes of Alexander Mackenzie's two great but almost forgotten expeditions.

47

All was not quiet along the Potomac early in 1862. The 28th Pennsylvania Volunteer Regiment, under command of Colonel John W. Geary of Kansas fame, was guarding a 24-mile stretch of the river, and there were occasional skirmishes between the opposing armies. On February 7, Geary shelled Harpers Ferry, and a few weeks later marched in and recaptured the town from the Confederates.

At some time between January 2 and February 24, 1862, somewhere along the shores of the Potomac, one of the unknown Confederate soldiers who was killed in these minor skirmishes may have been the world's first victim of machine-gun fire. Geary's regiment had two strange-looking new weapons into which cylindrical steel containers loaded with Minié balls, powder charges, and primed with percussion caps, were fed through a hopper while the single-barreled gun was operated by a hand crank. The new weapon, whose inventor is now unknown, was officially named the Union Repeating Gun but everyone, including President Lincoln, who had urged the Army to adopt it, called it the "coffee-mill" gun because it looked like an old-fashioned coffee grinder.

Geary's machine guns were first fired in actual battle in the Shenandoah Valley at Middleburg, Virginia, on March 29. A few weeks later an army officer, speaking in New York at Cooper Union, said: "One of these guns was brought to bear on a squadron of cavalry at 800 yards, and it cut them to pieces terribly, forcing them to fly." But Geary was not satisfied with the new guns' performance, finding them "inefficient and unsafe to the operators," so he returned them to the Washington Arsenal, where they were later disposed of as old metal for eight dollars each.

Lincoln's efforts to persuade his slow-thinking, slow-moving Army Ordnance Department to adopt more modern weapons have been described by Robert V. Bruce in *Lincoln and the Tools of War*. After the failure of the coffee-mill gun Lincoln stopped backing machine guns and concentrated on repeating rifles. But inventors kept working on the problem which had fascinated mechanically minded men ever since Leonardo da Vinci had made a sketch for a multi-barreled "organ gun." In 1718 an Englishman named James Puckle was granted a patent for what, on paper, looks like a workable machine gun. But since Puckle's patent drawing shows that his gun was supposed to fire round bullets against Christians and square ones against infidels, there is some doubt about his seriousness.

The problem kept tantalizing inventors for years, and some of them came up with ingenious—but not very practicable—solutions for it. One truly remarkable patent was granted in 1863 to James O. Whitcomb of New York for a four-barreled rapid-fire gun which was designed to be fired electrically. It was an intricate bit of mechanism which required split-second tuning that would never have stood up under battlefield conditions. The gun never got beyond the patent-drawing stage, but the inventor's boldness of thinking put him far ahead of his time.

The Confederates, too, became interested in the machine gun. One of them, Captain D. R. Williams, of Covington, Kentucky, built a rather clumsy repeating one-pounder that was first used at the Battle of Seven Pines (or Fair Oaks) on May 31 and June 1, 1862. Several batteries of these guns saw service during the war.

DOCTOR GATLING AND

A few other primitive rapid-fire guns were used by the Confederates in isolated instances. One of them, a forerunner of the famous Lewis machine gun of the First World War, was invented by the father of William C. Gorgas, whose sanitary work in suppressing yellow fever made the digging of the Panama Canal possible.

The first practical machine gun, the quick-firing weapon that was to change the tactics of warfare throughout the entire world, was invented by a southerner, Dr. Richard J. Gatling, who had been born in North Carolina but who later moved to the North. His father had been an inventor before him, and Gatling kept creating new devices all his long life.

Like many other inventors of deadly weapons who believed that they could discourage the human race from fighting by making warfare ever more terrible, Gatling considered his motives humanitarian. In a letter written twelve years after the Civil War he said: "In 1861 . . . (residing at the time in Indianapolis, Ind.) I witnessed almost daily the departure of troops to the front and the return of the wounded, sick and dead: The most of the latter lost their lives, not in battle, but by sickness and exposure incident to the service. It occurred to me if I could invent a machine—a gun—which could by its rapidity of fire, enable one man to do as much battle duty as a hundred, that it

Professing humanitarian motives,

he gave gangsters a word for their artillery

and the world its first practicable machine gun

HIS GUN

By PHILIP VAN DOREN STERN

Dr. Richard J. Gatling had this photograph of himself taken in Hartford, Connecticut, in 1893 with a very late model of his famous machine gun, rigged out with the Accles feed drum.

The Union Repeating Gun, popularly known as the "coffee mill," (below), was probably the first machine gun ever to kill a man in battle, a Confederate who fell in a skirmish along the Potomac in early 1862. Lincoln himself had backed the new device against a reluctant War Department. At the right a ten-barrel naval model appears on the deck of the U.S.S. Alliance while the officers and a lone enlisted man seem to be preparing to go into a few bars from H.M.S. Pinafore.

would, to a great extent, supersede the necessity of large armies, and consequently, exposure to battle and disease be greatly diminished."

This early proponent of push-button warfare went to work and by November 4, 1862, was granted his first patent for a machine gun with six revolving barrels turned by a crank. Since his first model, like the coffee-mill gun, used loaded steel containers, it was an improvement over that pioneer weapon only in that its multi-barrel principle kept the Gatling from overheating or from going out of commission if one barrel jammed. When Gatling redesigned his gun to take the newly developed metallic cartridge his weapon became the highly efficient, death-dealing machine that eventually was to make its inventor rich and famous. He finally reached popular immortality in gangsters' speech in which any repeating hand weapon became, by the linguistic process known as apocope, a "gat."

But the Gatling gun was so slow to win acceptance by the Army Ordnance Department that it never became important in the Civil War. The few Gatlings used saw service only because individual commanders procured them—sometimes with private funds.

Ben Butler was one of these commanders. He got a dozen Gatlings for his troops, and at least one of them is said to have been in action at Petersburg in the spring of 1865. (A very early Gatling gun bearing Serial No. 2, now in the West Point Museum, is probably one of the guns Butler bought.) The Navy was generally more progressive in its attitude toward new weapons than the Army, and Admiral David Dixon Porter ordered a Gatling sent to Cairo, Illinois. The Gatling gun's usefulness in protecting boats and bridges was quickly appreciated, and records show that they were mounted on various kinds of watercraft and at bridgeheads. Three of them were brought to New York to guard the New York *Times* building on Park Row during the bloody Draft Riots of July, 1863.

On February 18, 1864, Gatling wrote to Lincoln to explain the virtues of his gun and to ask for his assistance in getting it put to wider use. But by this time the harassed President had lost interest in machine guns. And in a few weeks he was to hand over the responsibility of deciding about the Union Army's strategy and equipment to Ulysses S. Grant. Lincoln therefore ignored Gatling's letter, and the gun lost its chance of turning the tide of battle in the Civil War.

Some of the first Gatling guns ever officially accepted by the U.S. Army were photographed (left) at the Washington Arsenal on the Potomac in 1866. Below them is one of the Gatlings that helped America win the Spanish-American War. Below: The Army has now come full circle, for the gun on the stand at the left is the very latest model ultra-rapid-fire machine gun, the Vulcan, which embodies many features of the old hand-operated Gatling gun beside it.

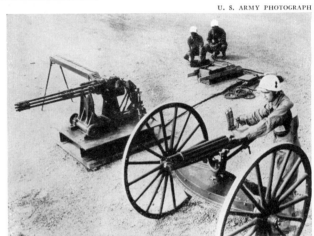

But perhaps the real reason why the Gatling gun did not have more influence on Civil War history is that its southern-born inventor was found to be a member of the secret Copperhead organizations that were threatening to take over the border and north-central states for the Confederacy. It was revealed, too, that he was offering his weapon for sale to anyone who would buy it—and this meant not only foreign governments but the Confederacy as well. One can hardly blame Gatling, who had been constantly rebuffed by the Army Ordnance Department, but he became very unpopular with American military men until the war was over. Then, on August 24, 1866, the Gatling gun was officially adopted by the United States Army, which ordered 100 of them. Gatling had these built by the Colt Patent Fire Arms Company, which manufactured all his guns from then on.

Once the official seal of American governmental approval was placed on his weapon, Gatling was in a good position to sell it to foreign countries. He did fairly well with the British, the Austrians, with various South American governments, and with the Russians (who called the gun the Gorloff after the general who adopted it), but he could not interest the French,

who were busy inventing their own mitrailleuse.

This French volley gun with 25 stationary barrels using paper cartridges was based on an entirely different principle from Gatling's revolving gun, and it was developed under such great secrecy that when it was sent into battle during the Franco-Prussian War of 1870, the soldiers who were supposed to use it had never been taught how to operate it. As a result the German armies rolled over France, and rapid-firing weapons were looked at skeptically by the military experts of the world for a generation to come. Among those who saw the failure of the French mitrailleuse in battle was General Philip H. Sheridan.

In 1876, when one of Sheridan's close personal friends and top cavalry commanders, General George A. Custer, led more than 250 doomed men of the famous 7th Cavalry into the Montana hill country to search for hostile Sioux Indians, he left behind a battery of Gatlings. If he had taken the then greatly improved machine guns with him the outcome of the much-discussed battle at the Little Big Horn would surely have been very different. But Custer thought that the wheeled gun carriages drawn by the condemned horses assigned to them would slow him down

CONTINUED ON PAGE 105

Whither the Course

In five dramatic allegorical paintings, Thomas Cole echoed the fear of Americans,

over a century ago, that all civilizations, our own included, must someday perish

Shortly before his death James Fenimore Cooper left off scolding his countrymen long enough to heap praises on the memory of his late friend Thomas Cole. Not only was Cole "the highest genius this country has ever produced" but also, in Cooper's estimation, his *The Course of Empire*, the series of five paintings reproduced on these pages, was "one of the noblest works of art ever wrought." He went on to predict that these canvases would one day be valued at fifty thousand dollars. In today's booming art market and with today's inflated prices that figure seems modest enough. But it was ten or twenty times larger than the artist's original fee and a far higher sum than any American painting had yet sold for.

Cooper was not, of course, a specialized critic or historian of art, neither of which is given to such unambiguous opinions about modern painting. But he was a sophisticate among his fellow Americans. Earlier in his life he had spent seven years in Europe where he himself had been accepted as a New World genius. (One thinks of Franz Schubert calling from his death bed for more of Cooper's novels to read.) He had honed his critical temper to a fine edge against the opinions and practices of the Old World, and he had gone shopping for "old masters" along the way.

Shortly after his return to America in 1833, the *Knickerbocker Magazine* somewhat caustically reminded American patrons of the arts that not every painting entering the country tagged with a big name was what it purported to be, and that they might better spend their money on works by the rising American artists of the day, such as Cole and Durand. Cooper needed no such encouragement; he was more at home with the artists than with the literary men of his own time and patronized them—Cole among others—both with advice and with commissions. It is part of his legend that he sat for long afternoons in the Louvre, "as regularly as the day comes," while Samuel F. B. Morse copied paintings in the Grande Galerie, ex-

claiming, "Lay it on here Samuel—more yellow—the nose is too short—the eye too small—damn it if I had been a painter what a picture I should have painted." Even so, the two remained lifelong friends.

The "glorious Fenimore" was by no means alone in his admiration of Cole's work in general and of *The Course of Empire* in particular. William Cullen Bryant, whose remarks to his compatriots at large were more cordially and respectfully received than Cooper's, had already labeled Cole a rare genius and had pronounced these five paintings "among the most remarkable and characteristic of his works." There was, in fact, no audible voice to the contrary at the time. When *The Course of Empire* was first shown to the public at the National Academy of Design in 1836 it was an immediate popular success, which merely enhanced Cole's already towering reputation in America.

After more than a century Cole's reputation as an artist is still secure; or, more exactly, it has been reestablished at a fairly high level. He was born in England in 1801 and was virtually self-taught. His latent talent had apparently been sparked in Ohio, whither he had moved with his family when he was nineteen, by a meeting with an itinerant portrait painter—possibly the same wandering artist who a few years later gave Audubon pointers in oil painting. By his middle twenties he had already won the respect of the professionals. "This youth," remarked the aging John Trumbull when he spotted some of Cole's early canvases in a New York store window, "has done what all my life I have attempted in vain." He bought a picture and persuaded his friends to buy others.

Cole went on to produce some of the most satisfying landscapes that were painted in America in his time. He was, to be sure, the leader and the most articulate member of the Hudson River School of painters, whose canvases—virtually by popular demand—opened up to Americans a fresh vision of their land. The country was clamoring for an art of its own, something

# of Empire?

By MARSHALL DAVIDSON

that would suggest the richness of its expectations and, quite specifically, the glory of its unique natural resources.

Cole was something of a writer as well as a painter. Before he won fame as an artist one of his stories had been published in the *Saturday Evening Post*, and all his life he wrote highly commendable verse. He often volunteered elaborate literary expositions to accompany his pictures, a practice most modern artists scorn until they are properly approached. He never doubted that his foremost purpose was to edify his contemporaries and to "improve posterity" with the spiritual content of his message. The colors and arrangements

TEXT CONTINUED ON PAGE 54

I THE SAVAGE STAGE
OR THE COMMENCEMENT OF EMPIRE

In his program for the series of five paintings, Cole wrote his patron, Luman Reed, that this first picture of The Course of Empire *"must be a view of a wilderness,—the sun rising from the sea, and the clouds of night retiring over the mountains. The figures must be savage, clothed in skins, and occupied in the chase. There must be a flashing chiaroscuro, and the spirit of motion pervading the scene, as though nature were just springing from chaos." The mist and clouds pull away from the landscape like a rising curtain, revealing the bay and the mountain "of peculiar form" in center stage—the fixed points of reference in Cole's drama.*

53

II THE ARCADIAN OR PASTORAL STATE

"The second picture must be the pastoral state,—the day further advanced—light clouds playing about the mountains —the scene partly cultivated—a rude village near the bay— small vessels in the harbour—groups of peasants either pursuing their labours in the field, watching their flocks, or engaged in some simple amusement. . . ." In the finished paintings Cole stayed fairly close to these original proposals. To vary his effects he changed the spectator's point of view from scene to scene. Here the enduring mountain has been shifted to the left of the stage. A rudimentary temple—a restored Stonehenge—replaces the primitive wigwams on the promontory. Man retains his early innocence; in the left foreground a philosopher traces his geometric abstractions with a stick; at far right, a shepherd pipes his tune for a couple of dancing Arcadians; in between, among other things, a child scratches out his fresh vision on a slab of rock and a female figure totes her distaff down a flowered path.

TEXT CONTINUED FROM PAGE 53

of his canvases were important, not so much in themselves, but as aids to his preachments. That approach to art has become singularly unfashionable. Nowadays the abstract elements of a painting are considered not only of primary importance, but, at the extreme of current practice, quite enough in themselves without any recognizable content.

In spite of our contrary-mindedness about these matters, *The Course of Empire* has quite recently been rated by one critic "the most extraordinary series of paintings in American art." It may well be. In the five pictures there are what the professionals term "some delightful passages," particularly in the last of the series, "The Ruins of Empire," where the artist levels off from the histrionic flights of the preceding subjects and, with the tension relieved, concludes his story with quiet dignity. Taken individually, each of the canvases has painterly merits which few of his American contemporaries could have matched. But they labor under the allegorical freight with which Cole burdened his message.

He was hardly cold in his grave before the critics started complaining of the heavy, ethical weight of his allegories. But it is just this which for us, a century later, makes this series such an important cultural landmark. The historical place of any work of art remains an abiding fact in our enjoyment of it. Even masterpieces long and universally celebrated as the very standards of beauty are to a degree also objects of knowledge about the past. *The Course of Empire,* whatever its other qualities, is an outstanding historical monument.

The series had been painted on commission for Luman Reed, one of New York's most distinguished and liberal patrons of art. It was originally intended to all but cover one wall of Reed's private art gallery in his Greenwich Street residence. Reed died shortly before Cole completed the project and the five paintings found their way to the New-York Historical Society, where they hang today in monumental splendor. The patron had given the artist his choice of subject and Cole came up with an elaborate program that seems to have been accepted without serious modification.

"A series of pictures might be painted," he wrote

TEXT CONTINUED ON PAGE 58

(OVERLEAF)   III   THE CONSUMMATION OF EMPIRE

"The third must be a noonday,—a great city girding the bay, gorgeous piles of architecture, bridges, aqueducts, temples—the port crowded with vessels—splendid processions, &c.—all that can be combined to show the fulness of prosperity: the chiaroscuro broad." This painting, with which Cole reaches the climax of his theme, is larger than the others. For the passing moment of human triumph, the mountain has been withdrawn almost in the wings at the right. Front stage is occupied by the conqueror, astride an elephant, returning to a hero's welcome. Cole practically exhausted his rich architectural vocabulary in staging this scene—and his imagination as well, for the time. Here is the Classic Revival, literally, with a vengeance. Before finishing all this "gaud and glitter" he switched to the fifth picture for a respite. But with the city finally built on the canvas, he might have observed, as H. G. Wells is said to have done on his first view of New York's sky line: "What a magnificent ruins it will make!"

55

TEXT CONTINUED FROM PAGE 54

Reed in September, 1833, "that should illustrate the history of a natural scene, as well as be an epitome of Man,—showing the natural changes of landscape, and those effected by man in his progress from barbarism to civilization—to luxury—to the vicious state, or state of destruction—and to the state of ruin and desolation.

"The philosophy of my subject is drawn from the history of the past, wherein we see how nations have risen from the savage state to that of power and glory, and then fallen, and become extinct. Natural scenery has also its changes,—the hours of the day and the seasons of the year—sunshine and storm: these justly applied will give expression to each picture of the series I would paint. It will be well to have the same location in each picture: this location be identified by the introduction of some striking object in each scene —a mountain of peculiar form, for instance. This will not in the least preclude variety. The scene must be composed so as to be picturesque in its wild state, appropriate for cultivation, and the site of a sea-port.

"The fourth should be a tempest,—a battle, and the burning of a city—towers falling, arches broken, vessels wrecking in the harbour. In this scene there should be a fierce chiaroscuro, masses and groups swaying about like stormy waves. This is the scene of destruction or vicious state." The dream of empire has become a surrealistic nightmare. Pillage, fire, tempest, rape, and murder reduce man and his proudest works to a shambles. Here again, the artist was hard put to stay with his theme. *"For my part,"* he wrote his patron at one point, *"I have been engaged in sacking and burning a city ever since I saw you, and I am well tired of such horrible work."* The headless statue of a gladiator stands as a symbol of futile defiance to the inevitable course of empire. The mountain, now in the center background, remains serenely above the tumult.

There must be the sea, a bay, rocks, waterfalls and woods. . . ."

His synopsis of the five episodes that would comprise his great cycle is quoted in the captions for the accompanying illustrations. It was a grandiose concept that called for an indulgent patron as well as for a tireless and consecrated artist. "You will perceive," Cole concluded in his letter, "what an arduous task I have set myself. . . ."

It takes some effort to bear in mind that the most

discerning and best informed Americans of the time were apparently deeply moved by this allegorical extravaganza when it was first shown to the world three years later. To find a modern version of what now seems such obvious sentiment and melodramatic imagery we must turn to Hollywood's epic spectaculars. The analogy comes quickly to mind, for Cole was undoubtedly influenced by those vast "wide-angle" panoramic canvases that enjoyed such a great vogue in the nineteenth century, and that in their developed form, winding off one cylinder and onto another before delighted audiences, were in fact called "moving pictures." The fourth of Cole's paintings is indeed very closely related to one of the more popular panoramas of the day, Robert Burford's *Pandemonium from Milton's Paradise Lost.*

However, the fact that Cole's "cosmoramic" performance was applauded by the most sensitive critics of his generation involves no real paradox, merely a shift of historical viewpoint. Over the century that has elapsed since Cole first showed these canvases, Spengler and Toynbee, a host of archaeological revelations, two world wars, and the most recent disturbances at Yucca Flats have made us intimately familiar with the uneasy thought that human societies, like human beings, are perishable; a thought that was so simply and admirably summarized for our own time in James Thurber's cartoon sequence, *The Last Flower.*

We have lived long and closely enough with the theme to accept it as presented by the cartoonist's shorthand. But to Cole's generation it had the enchantment of novelty. As late children of the Renaissance Americans were quite aware of their continuous line of descent from the ancient Greeks and Romans. The world still seemed very young. There was, in fact, lingering authority in Bishop Ussher's pronouncement that it had been created in 4004 B.C. When

Charles Willson Peale unearthed the first mastodon skeletons near Newburgh, in 1801, this awesome revelation of a prehistory caused international excitement. Even Thomas Jefferson, as Edgar Richardson observes, first resisted the thought that "Nature's God" could allow one of his own creations to disappear; and he posted Lewis and Clark to keep an eye out for specimens in the uncharted West.

America had read with fascination Constantin Volney's *Les Ruines; ou méditations sur les révolutions des empires,* which told of great civilizations of a remote, strange past that had actually vanished from earth. Volney was a wandering French intellectual who had adventured into the mysterious deserts of the Near East and reported the almost unheard-of ruins he saw there—ruins of some civilizations more ancient than those of Greece or Rome.

While Cole was painting his series, the *Knickerbocker Magazine* was running the stories of John Lloyd Stephens, an American who had penetrated more deeply than Volney into exotic lands of quite forgotten history. Stephens had gone to Mycenae, the Holy Lands, Arabia Petraea, and other far reaches of the world before he plunged into the wilderness of Central America and described the weird remains of high civilizations that had once flourished on our own continent and had long since disappeared beneath the jungle. He was a superb adventure writer and his tales fired the imagination of his generation.

The American mind, so long and comfortably rooted in the classic tradition of Greece and Rome, was getting a disturbing new vision of the past. Was it possible that the course of empire was not to be as Bishop Berkeley had predicted the century before?

Westward the course of empire takes its way;
The four first acts already past,
  A fifth shall close the drama with the day:
Time's noblest offspring is the last.

Might a different ending be written for the fifth act? Cole himself had observed the ruins of ancient

V THE RUINS OF EMPIRE

"The fifth must be a sunset,—the mountains riven—the city a desolate ruin—columns standing isolated amid the encroaching waters—ruined temples, broken bridges, fountains, sarcophagi, &c.—no human figure—a solitary bird perhaps: a calm and silent effect. This picture must be as the funeral knell of departed greatness, and may be called the state of desolation." In this finished version of Cole's fifth stage of civilization THE mountain is not riven; it stands firm and in final judgment. In the evening of time's cycle a family of herons has taken over a broken ivied column that remains from man's presumption to improve on unspoiled nature with his monuments to human progress.

worlds in Sicily and at Paestum, Rome, and Volterra. Like so many of his artistic and literary countrymen he made his pilgrimages to the Old World as a professional "duty"; and, like the rest, he bore the impress of his experiences all his life. On the eve of the painter's first departure, Bryant, in a sonnet, counseled his friend and kindred spirit to gaze on the antique splendors of Europe "till the tears shall dim thy sight"; but to keep bright that "earlier, wilder image" of their beloved America. To impress that image of natural beauty more brightly on his mind, Cole made one last excursion into the wilderness just before he sailed away from home.

But at Volterra, perched on a cliffside, he shuddered with "awful delight" at the prospect before him. At home he had often mused on the brink of some rocky precipice "without thought of its indestructibility; but here the great mass, bearing the marks of rapid and continuous decay, awakened the instantaneous thought that it was perishable as a cloud." He practically exhausted the romanticist's vocabulary trying to describe his impressions. And as he sat under the ruin of an Etruscan wall, "gazing long and silently on the great scene of desolate sublimity," the theme for *The Course of Empire* took shape in his mind's eye.

The commission from Reed almost immediately followed the artist's return to America. It took him more than three years to complete the assignment, a time during which he himself occasionally tired of the gaud, the glitter, and the tumult which he felt obliged to put on canvas. During those same three years Ralph Waldo Emerson was preparing his first published work. *The Course of Empire* and *Nature* appeared almost simultaneously.

Of the two classics Cole's paintings probably won more immediate favorable attention. But Emerson's essay reduced to a statement of conviction the dilemma that not only haunted Cole's work but that bothered a whole generation of American artists and writers in one way or another. In one of his recent

pieces Perry Miller has dealt very suggestively with this question that led to so much unresolved confusion in the culture of nineteenth-century America—the obsessive drama, *the* American theme, he calls it, of Nature versus civilization.

Whatever the age of the rest of the world, America was in its glorious youth in the 1830's. After two generations of successful self-government and rising prosperity, it was prepared to tell the world that it held the key to the future. "We are pioneers of the world," Herman Melville declared in a moment of unrestrained optimism. "God has predestined, mankind expects, great things from our race; and great things we feel in our souls. The most of the nations must soon be in our rear. We are . . . the advance guard, sent on through the wilderness of untried things, to break a path in the New World that is ours." And to Melville, as to a multitude of others—Europeans as well as Americans—the national virtue which would make all things possible was a lavish gift of Nature. In the works of the landscape painters, the poems of Bryant, the novels of Cooper, and the exhortations of politicians, the very spirit of America was identified with its majestic wilderness preserves; at least with its diminishing remains where, as Hawthorne wrote, "the damned shadow of Europe" had not yet settled.

Emerson was the prophet of this romantic generation. His essay spoke quietly and wisely of those truths that seemed fundamental to the time. He opened a perspective wider and deeper than was visible to the chauvinists of the day; he was concerned with the large problems of human nature and of human destiny in general. And in Nature, he reminded the world, man finds all he knows and all he needs to know, a pronouncement with which Wordsworth, Goethe, and leading romanticists were in sympathy.

But in America Nature was not only a picturesque retreat for the romantic imagination, as we might say it was for Goethe and Wordsworth; it was also a stubborn, wild fact that had to be contended with on a continental scale. It was something that had to be reconciled, not with the hoary past of man, but with his illimitable future. By the eighteenth century, according to one foreign visitor, the American had developed an "unconquerable aversion" to the trees of the unending dark forest that hemmed him in at every turn; he cut all away before him without mercy—with positive delight, in fact. It was a practice that continued to horrify English visitors, particularly, until well into the nineteenth century. But Europe had not known forests on such a scale for countless centuries. To travel for days on end through a thick gloom among trees a hundred feet high was oppressing be-

CONTINUED ON PAGE 104

Esmeralda, Sept. 9, 1862

Dear Billy:

. . . It appears to me that the very *existence* of the United States is threatened just now. I am afraid we have been playing the game of brag about as recklessly as I have ever seen it played, even on an Arkansas steamboat—"going blind" and "doubling the pot" and "straddling" and "calling" on hands without a "pair," or even an "ace at the head." D——n it! only to think of this sickening boasting—these miserable self-complacent remarks about "twenty-four hours more will seal the fate of the bastard Confederacy—twenty-four hours more will behold the United States dictating terms to submissive and groveling rebeldom!" Great God! and at that very moment the national army were inaugurating a series of retreats more disastrous than bloody defeats on the battlefield! Think of it, my boy—last week the nation were blowing like school-boys of what they were going to do—this week they are trembling in their boots and whining and sniveling like threatened puppies—absolutely frantic with fear. God! what we were going to do! and last night's dispatches come to hand—we all rush to see what the mountain in labor hath brought forth, and lo! the armies have fled back to Washington; its very suburbs were menaced by the foe; Baton Rouge is evacuated; the rebel hosts march through Kentucky and occupy city after city without firing a gun. . . .

Mark Twain ca. 1859

Let us change the disgusting subject.—Let us close our eyes and endeavor to discover in these things profound, mysterious wonders of "strategy!" Ah me—I have often thought of it—what a crown of glory it would be to us to slip quietly out of Washington some night and when the rebels entered it in the morning, overwhelm them with the bitter humiliation that the whole transaction was a masterpiece of "strategy!" Strategy be d——d—all these astonishing feats of strategy which we have been treated to lately, and which we stared at with a stunned look, and dimly felt that it was a big thing—a wonderful thing—and said so in deadened tones bereft of inflection, although, to save our souls from being eternally damned we couldn't distinctly "see it" —all these "strategic" feats are beautiful—beautiful as early dawn—yet, like unto the mild and lovely juvenile show, "six pins admittance," they don't amount to a damn when the "shore-nuff" circus comes to town.

Strategy will bust this nation yet, if they just keep it up long enough, my boy. . . .   Your old friend,
                                                                            Sam L. C.

Two Civil

Hardly a person in America was untouched by the Civil War, and Mark Twain and Walt Whitman were no exceptions. Because they were perhaps the most distinctly "American" writers of their time, their reactions to the conflict are particularly interesting. Printed here are two of their wartime letters, both written within six months of each other, at a time when the North seemed on the verge of defeat. While Whitman's letter to his New York friends, Nat and Fred Gray, has appeared before, the Twain letter is a completely new find. Both are owned by the noted book collector, Clifton Waller Barrett, and AMERICAN HERITAGE publishes them through his courtesy.

The Civil War was a crisis which Twain and Whitman observed as civilians—but then, the number of important American writers who saw active service is surprisingly small. Men like Emerson, Hawthorne, Lowell, Melville, and Whitman—the established talents—were all too old to fight. Many of the younger group who grew up during the war managed to avoid it, whether intentionally or otherwise.

Mark Twain (or Samuel Clemens, to use his real name) chose not to fight and went West instead; for non-participation was his answer to the dilemma of divided allegiance. It is true that he did join a hastily organized Confederate militia company in Missouri late in the spring of 1861—an adventure in war which began "full of horse-play and school-boy hilarity," and ended as an inglorious retreat in the rain from an enemy who was reported everywhere and was nowhere seen. If Twain's fine story, "A Private History of a Campaign That Failed," can be believed, a senseless tragedy in which he participated spoiled his stomach for military life once and for all. One night Twain and some panicky companions shot and killed a lone rider whom they mistook for a Union soldier, only to discover that the man was an innocent traveler.

When his older brother, Orion Clemens, offered him a chance to go west that summer, Twain readily accepted. Orion, a staunch Union supporter and an abolitionist, had been lately appointed secretary of the Nevada Territory; under his influence Twain came to accept the Northern viewpoint, although remaining

War Letters

aloof to the war itself. In all that he wrote during his five years in the West as a miner and newspaper reporter, he rarely even mentioned it. One of the few exceptions is his letter to an erstwhile mining companion, Billy Clagett, written in September, 1862, soon after the Union disaster at the second battle of Bull Run. At that moment it seemed to Twain—as it did to so many—that the very existence of the United States was threatened.

Six months later and a thousand miles closer to the war, Walt Whitman in Washington could view the situation with greater confidence, even though the fortunes of the North remained at a low ebb after another costly defeat at Fredericksburg in December. But something he saw in the military hospitals of the capital—something Twain could not see from his western remove—convinced Whitman that the Union would stand the test. He had come to regard the war as the indeed irrepressible and even necessary fire-tempering ordeal of democracy; thus the measure of survival was the nation's ability to pass beyond the horizon of durable anguish—as he expressed it in his letter to the Gray brothers, "how certain man, our American man . . . holds himself cool and unquestioned master above all pains and bloody mutilations."

Whitman was one of the few writers of his generation who had any direct contact with the war. When his younger brother was wounded at Fredericksburg, he had gone to Washington to search for him; there he remained to work as a kind of unofficial nurse and comforter in the military hospitals.

Patriarchal in appearance with his prematurely gray beard, this large, slow-moving man became a familiar sight to the wounded and dying in the vast, crowded wards. Each day he would visit them, carrying a knapsack filled with oranges, candy, tobacco, writing paper, and stamps. "I believe," he wrote, "that even the moving around among the men, or through the ward, of a hearty, healthy, clean, strong, generous-souled person . . does immense good." As Van Wyck Brooks points out, it was an opportunity to measure as never before the American people en masse, and the view that resulted was as confident as Twain's was pessimistic.

Washington, March 19, 1863.

Dear Nat, and Fred Gray:

Since I left New York, I was down in the Army of the Potomac in front with my brother a good part of the winter, commencing time of the battle of Fredericksburgh—have seen war-life, the real article—folded myself in a blanket, lying down in the mud with composure—relished salt pork & hard tack—have been on the battle field among the wounded the faint and the bleeding, to give them nourishment—have gone over with a flag of truce the next day to help direct the burial of the dead—have struck up a tremendous friendship with a young Mississippi Captain, (about 19) that we took prisoner badly wounded at Fredericksburgh—(he has followed me here, is in Emory hospital here, minus a leg—he wears his Confederate uniform, proud as the devil—I met him first at Falmouth, in the Lacy house, middle of December last, his leg just cut off, and cheered him up—poor boy, he has suffered a great deal, and still suffers—has eyes bright as a hawk, but face pale—sometimes when I lean over to say I am going, he puts his arm round my neck, draws my face down, etc. quite a scene for the New Bowery.) I spent Christmas holidays on the Rappahannock.

Walt Whitman ca. 1863

During January came up hither, took a lodging room here, did the 37th Congress, especially the night sessions the last three weeks, explored the Capitol then, meandering the gorgeous painted interminable senate corridors, getting lost in them, (a new sensation, rich & strong, that endless painted interior at night,) got very much interested in some particular cases in Hospitals here, go now steadily to more or less of said Hospitals by day or night. . . .

These Hospitals, so different from all others, these thousands, and tens and twenties of thousands of American young men, badly wounded, all sorts of wounds, operated on, pallid with diarrhea, languishing, dying with fever, pneumonia, &c. open a new world somehow to me, giving closer insights, new things, exploring deeper mines than any yet, showing our humanity, (I sometimes put myself in fancy in the cot, with typhoid, or under the knife) tried by terrible, fearfulest tests, probed deepest, the living soul's, the body's tragedies, bursting the petty bonds of art. To these, what are your dramas and poems, even the oldest and tearfulest? Not old Greek mighty ones, where man contends with fate, (and always yields) not Virgil showing Dante on and on among the agonized & damned, approach what here I see and take a part in. For here I see, not at intervals, but quite always, how certain man, our American man, how he holds himself cool and unquestioned master above all pains and bloody mutilations. It is immense, the best thing of all, nourishes me of all men. This then, what frightened us all so long! Why it is put to flight with ignominy, a mere stuffed scarecrow of the fields.

O death where is thy sting? O grave where is thy victory? etc. In the Patent Office, as I stood there one night, just off the cot-side of a dying soldier, in a large ward that had received the worst cases of 2d Bull Run, Antietam and Fredericksburgh, the surgeon, Dr. Stone, (Horatio Stone, the sculptor,) told me, of all who had died in that crowded ward the past six months, he had still to find the first man or boy who had met the approach of death with a single tremor, or unmanly fear.

But let me change the subject. . . . Washington and its points I find bear a second and a third perusal, and doubt-less indeed many. My first impressions, architectural, &c. were not favorable; but upon the whole, the city, the spaces, buildings, &c. make no unfit emblem of our country, so far, so broadly planned, every thing in plenty, money & materials staggering with plenty, but the fruit of the plans, the knit, the combination yet wanting. Determined to express ourselves greatly in a Capital but no fit Capital yet here, (time, associations wanting, I suppose) many a hiatus yet, many a thing to be taken down and done over again yet, perhaps an entire change of base, may-be a succession of changes. Congress does not seize very hard upon me, I studied it and its members with curiosity . . . much gab, great fear of public opinion, plenty of low business talent, but no masterful man in Congress, (probably best so).

I think well of the President. He has a face like a Hoosier Michael Angelo, so awful ugly it becomes beautiful, with its strange mouth, its deep cut, criss-cross lines, and its doughnut complexion. My notion is too, that underneath his outside smutched mannerism, and stories from third-class county bar-rooms, (it is his humor,) Mr. Lincoln keeps a fountain of first-class practical telling wisdom. I do not dwell on the supposed failures of his government; he has shown, I sometimes think an almost supernatural tact in keeping the ship afloat at all, with head steady, not only not going down, and now certain not to, but with proud and resolute spirit, and flag flying in sight of the world, menacing and high as ever. I say never yet captain, never ruler, had such a perplexing dangerous task as his, the past two years. I more and more rely upon his idiomatic western genius, careless of court dress or court decorums.

I am living here without much definite aim (except going to the hospitals,) yet I have quite a good time. I make some money by scribbling for the papers, and as copyist. I have had, (and have,) thoughts of trying to get a clerkship or something, but I only try in a listless sort of way, and of course do not succeed. I have strong letters of introduction from Mr. [Ralph Waldo] Emerson to Mr. Seward and Mr. Chase, but I have not presented them. I have seen Mr. Sumner several times anent of my office-hunting, he promised fair once, but he does not seem to be finally fascinated. I hire a bright little 3d story front room, with service, &c. for $7 a month, dine in the same house, (394 L St. a private house,) and remain yet much of the old vagabond that so gracefully becomes me. . . . My health, strength, personal beauty, etc. are I am happy to inform you, without diminution, but on the contrary quite the reverse. I weigh full 220 pounds avoirdupois, yet still retain my usual perfect shape, a regular model. My beard, neck, &c. are woolier, fleecier, whiteyer than ever. . . .

Friday Morning. 20th. I finish my letter in the office of Major Hapgood, a paymaster and a friend of mine. This is a large building, filled with paymaster's offices some thirty or forty or more. This room is up on the fifth floor (a most noble and broad view from my window.) Curious scenes around here, a continual stream of soldiers, officers, cripples, etc. etc. some climbing wearily up the stairs. They seek their pay, and every hour, almost every minute, has its incident, its hitch, its romance, farce or tragedy. There are two paymasters in this room. A sentry at the street door, another half way up the stairs, another at the chief clerk's door, all with muskets & bayonets, sometimes a great swarm, hundreds, around the sidewalk in front waiting. (Everybody is waiting for something here.) I take a pause, look up, a couple of minutes from my pen and paper, see spread, off there, the Potomac, very fine, nothing petty about it, the Washington monument, not half finished, the public grounds around it filled with ten thousand beeves on the hoof, to the left the Smithsonian with its brown turrets, to the right, far across, Arlington heights, the forts, eight or ten of them, then the long bridge, and down a ways, but quite plain, the shipping of Alexandria, opposite me, and in stone throw, is the Treasury building, and below the bustle and life of Pennsylvania Avenue. I shall hasten with my letter, and then go forth and take a stroll down "the avenue" as they call it here.

Now you boys, don't you think I have done the handsome thing by writing this astounding, magnificent letter, certainly the longest I ever wrote in my life? . . .

Walt

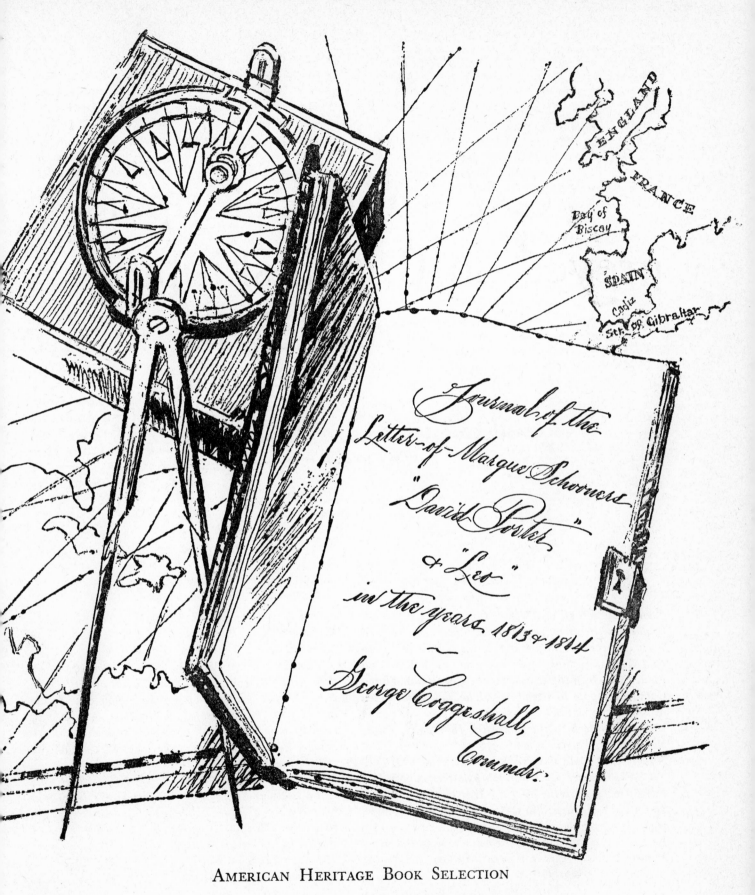

Journal of the
Letter-of-Marque Schooners
"David Porter"
& "Leo"
in the years 1813 & 1814
~
George Coggeshall,
Commdr.

AMERICAN HERITAGE BOOK SELECTION

ILLUSTRATED FOR AMERICAN HERITAGE BY DAVID STONE

$\mathcal{A}$ Yankee skipper who preyed on British shipping relates his wartime

George Coggeshall of Milford, Connecticut, was a sea captain in the great Yankee tradition. His father had been a successful shipmaster but was ruined by repeated confiscations of his cargoes by British and French vessels in the years after the Revolution. Young George, too poor to attend school, had been sent to sea as soon as he was old enough to carry a message from the quarter-deck to the forecastle. In 1809, when he was only 25, he received his first command and altogether spent some sixty years of his life at sea.

Like so many American shipmasters, Coggeshall turned to privateering after the War of 1812 began. It was a risky business, but a profitable one if managed right. With regular channels of trade closed by hostilities, it was a financial necessity for most shipowners. During the war years American privateers ranged the oceans of the world from the Bay of Biscay to the China Sea and captured some 1,350 prizes. By 1814 privateers were bagging an average of three merchant-

men a day. In fact, they did more actual damage to British shipping than the much-publicized American Navy.

The two vessels which Coggeshall commanded in these troubled times, the David Porter and the Leo, were known as letter-of-marque schooners. While armed and commissioned to capture and destroy enemy commerce, they differed from conventional privateers in the respect that they carried cargoes and sailed for more or less set destinations.

Thirty years after the war, Captain Coggeshall, who had a lively pen and an eye for interesting detail, put his memories and old logbooks together in book form. AMERICAN HERITAGE is happy to be able to print here certain of the more exciting portions of his wartime adventures, taken directly, with very slight modernizations in the text, from the original Coggeshall manuscript, now in the possession of Colonel A. C. M. Azoy of Ardsley-on-Hudson, New York.

experiences

At this period of the war [the fall of 1813] there were but three ways for captains of merchant ships to find employment in their ordinary vocations: namely, enter the United States Navy as sailing masters, go privateering, or command a letter-of-marque—carry a cargo and, as it were, force trade and fight their way or run, as the case might be; and thus, as the last alternative I chose the latter.

I gave myself some weeks of leisure, and then consulted a few friends on the subject of purchasing a pilot-boat schooner and going into the French trade. After looking about for a suitable vessel, I at length met with a fine schooner of about 200 tons burthen, called the *David Porter*. She was built in Milford, my native town, and had made but one voyage, namely, from New York to St. Jean de Luz, France, from thence to St. Bartholomew, and from that place to Providence, R.I., where she then lay. She was a fine, fast-sailing vessel, and tolerably well armed, namely, a long 18-pounder on a pivot amidships, four 6-pounders, with muskets, pistols, etc. I purchased one half of this schooner for $6,000 from the former owners in Milford, Connecticut. They retained the other half for their own account. My New York friends, Messrs. Lawrence and Whitney, and James Lovett, Esq., bought one quarter, and I retained the other quarter for my own account.

We finally decided on a voyage from Providence to Charleston, S.C., and from thence to France under my command. I forthwith proceeded to Providence and arrived at that place on the 21st of October, 1813. Here I purchased 1,500 bushels of salt, and after getting the salt on board we filled up the vessel with potatoes, butter, cheese, etc., the whole cargo amounting to $3,500. I took with me as first lieutenant my former mate in the *Canton*, Mr. Samuel Nichols, Joseph Anthony 2nd lieutenant and Charles Coggeshall 3rd lieutenant, with a complement of about 30 petty officers and men. My boatswain, carpenter and gunner, with several of the men, had just been discharged from the frigate *President* and were very efficient and good men.

I left Providence on the 10th of November with a fine fresh gale from the N.N.W., and in a few hours got down to Newport, there to lie a few days to get ready for sea and wait a favorable time to go out the harbor, that is to say, a dark night and a N.E. snow storm; for in these days to avoid the vigilance of the enemy we were obliged to wait for dark stormy nights to leave or enter our ports. On the morning of the 14th I met with a New York friend, and to this gentleman I committed what little treasure I had left after getting ready for sea. The whole consisted of 30 gold guineas, sundry bank notes and my gold watch, with a request that he would stop at Stamford, Connecticut, on his way to New York, and leave the above-mentioned articles with my sister.

At this time there was a British 74 and a frigate cruising off the harbor of Newport to blockade the port and watch the movements of the United States frigate *President,* which ship was then lying at Providence.

Towards evening on the 16th of November, I got under weigh, with the wind at E.N.E. At this time no vessel was permitted to go to sea without first presenting a clearance to the commanding officer at the outer fort, at the entrance to the harbor. Consequently, I ran down near the fort just before dark and, for fear of any mistake or detention, took my papers and went myself to the commanding officer and got permission to pass the fort by exhibiting a lantern in the main shrouds for a few minutes. It soon commenced snowing, with a fresh gale at N.E. We ran rapidly out of the harbor and soon got outside of the blockading squadron, and now my greatest fear was running on to Block Island. Fortunately, however, at daylight we saw no land; neither was there a single sail in sight.

On the 17th of November was chased by a man-of-war brig. He being to windward, I hove off, and soon had the pleasure to run him out of sight. On the 24th off Georgetown, was chased all day by a man-of-war brig, with a schooner in company. They being to leeward, consequently I tacked and plied to windward and made good my retreat before night. I could have got into Georgetown the next day, but fearing my cargo would not sell as well as at Charleston, I stood on for that port.

November the 26th, at six o'clock, daylight, in 10 fathoms of water off Cape Romain, saw a man-of-war brig on our weather quarter [that is, to windward], distant about three miles. He soon made sail in chase; I kept wide off to leeward in hopes of drawing him down, so that I could weather him on the opposite tack. This manoeuvre did not succeed, as the enemy only kept off about four points. We both therefore maintained our relative positions, and the chase continued for four hours. I had determined not to run to leeward for fear of coming in contact with another foe, but to hug the wind and run in shore. At 10 A.M. I saw Charleston Lighthouse, bearing north, about ten miles distant. I set my ensign and hauled close upon the wind. This brought the enemy on my starboard beam at long gun-shot distance. I then fired my center gun but could not quite reach him, the wind being light from the northward. At half past ten, I gave him another shot, and though it did not take effect, with a spyglass I saw the shot dash water on his quarter.

I suppose the reason he did not fire was that he could not reach me with his carronades. At eleven, within five miles from Charleston Bar, I saw two schooners coming over the bar and bearing directly down upon the brig, when he squared his yards and ran away to leeward. The two schooners were the famous privateer *Decatur* of Charleston, with 7 guns, and a complement of over a hundred men; and the other schooner was the letter-of-marque *Adaline,* Capt. Craycroft of Philadelphia, bound to France. The schooners took no notice of the brig, hauled to the eastward and were soon out of sight. I crossed the bar and got up to Charleston without any further difficulty; and then I was told that the man-of-war brig was the *Dotterall,* carrying 18 guns.

[Coggeshall remained in Charleston for three weeks. There he disposed of the salt and foodstuffs at a good profit and took on a fresh cargo consisting of 331 bales of compressed cotton, 16 kegs of potash, and 25 tons of pig iron for ballast.]

The Congress of the United States had lately assembled at Washington, and great fears were entertained by many that an embargo would soon be laid. I was of course extremely anxious to get out of port, as such a measure would have been ruinous to myself and the other owners of my vessel and as it was impossible to get out over the bar while the wind was blowing strong directly into the harbor. I therefore, to avoid being stopped by an embargo and to keep my men on board, judged it best to drop as low down the harbor as possible and watch the first favorable moment to proceed to sea. Fortunately the weather cleared up the next day, and with a favorable breeze and fine weather I left the port of Charleston on the 20th of December, 1813, bound to Bordeaux.

I had a good run off the coast and met with nothing worth remarking until the 27th, namely about a week after leaving port, when I fell in with a small English brig from Jamaica, bound for Nova Scotia.

As it was about four o'clock in the afternoon, and at this time blowing a strong gale from the N.W. with a high sea running, I did not think it safe to board him until the gale should moderate and the sea became smoother, and therefore ordered him to carry as much sail as possible and follow me on our course to the eastward until better weather. He reluctantly followed, and once before dark I was obliged to hail and give him to understand that if he shewed too great a disposition to lag behind or did not carry all the sail his brig could bear, he would probably feel the effect of one of my stern guns. This had the desired effect and he followed kindly at a convenient distance until midnight, when it became very dark and squally and we soon after lost sight of our first prize, which I did not much regret, as I could not conveniently spare men enough to send him into port.

From this period until we got near the European coast, we scarcely saw a sail and did not meet with a single man-of-war. Thus while the whole coast of the United States was literally lined with English cruisers, on the broad ocean there were very few to be seen; a clear proof that the risk of capture between Newport and Charleston was infinitely greater than going to France.

At this period we were not obliged to deliver the goods on freight at any particular place or port, but to some port in France, even from one extreme of the empire to the other: as for example, anywhere on the western coast from St. Jean de Luz to Ostend.

My bills of lading were filled up upon this principle to Bordeaux or a port in France, and so that on the arrival of the goods, the owners or agents were bound to receive them at any port or place where the vessel was fortunate enough to enter. My object was to get as near Bordeaux as possible; still I did not like to attempt entering the Garonne, as the English generally kept stationed several frigates and smaller vessels directly off the Cordovan Light, which rendered it extremely difficult and hazardous to enter. I therefore decided to run for the harbor of Lateste.

About a week before we got into port, while in the Bay of Biscay, namely on the 19th and 20th of January, we encountered one of the most severe gales from the westward that I have ever experienced. It commenced early on the morning of the 19th and blew a perfect hurricane, which soon raised a high, cross sea. At 8 A.M., I hove the schooner to under a double reefed foresail, lowered down the foreyard near the deck and got everything as snug as possible. At 12 o'clock noon a tremendous sea struck her in the wake of the starboard fore-shrouds. The force of the sea broke one of the toptimbers or stanchions [uprights which support a ship's deck] and split open the plank-sheer [the heavy plank forming the outer edge of the deck] so that I could see directly into the hold. The force of the sea and the weight of the water that came on board threw the vessel nearly on her beam ends. Fortunately the weight of water that fell into the foresail split the sail and tore away the bulwarks; and being thus relieved, she gradually righted.

We then threw overboard two of the lee guns, water casks, etc., and after nailing tarred canvas and leather over the broken plank-sheer, got ready to wear ship [to change course by turning the stern to windward], fearing the injury received in the wake of the starboard fore-shrouds would endanger the foremast. We accordingly got ready to hoist a small piece of the mainsail, and thus kept her off before the wind for a few minutes, and watched a favorable smooth time to bring her to the wind on the other tack. During the time that the schooner ran before the wind she appeared literally to leap from one sea to another. We soon, however, brought her up to the wind on the other tack without accident, and thus under a small piece of the mainsail she lay to pretty well. But as the gale continued to rage violently, I feared we might ship another sea, and therefore prepared, as it were, to anchor the vessel head to the wind.

For this purpose we took a square sail boom, spanned it at each end with a new four-inch rope and made our small bower cable fast to the bight of the span; and with the other end fastened to the foremast, threw it overboard and payed out about 60 fathoms of cable. She then rode like a gull on the water, and I was absolutely astonished to see the good effect of this experiment. The spar broke the sea and kept the schooner nearly head to the wind until the gale subsided.

The next day in the afternoon, January 20th, we again made sail, and on the 26th, six days after this dreadful tempest, got safe into Lateste, 37 days from Charleston.

While we providentially escaped destruction, other ships were not so fortunate; many were wrecked and stranded along the coast, and five sail of English transports were thrown on shore near Lateste, and most of their crews perished in the same gale. On my arrival at Lateste, all my papers were sent up to Paris; and although we were all well, still we were compelled by the government to ride quarantine for six days.

Lateste is a poor little village principally supported by fish and oysters taken in its waters and sold in Bordeaux, from which city it is distant 30 miles and 56 miles from the mouth of the Garonne. With a bad sand bar at the mouth of the harbor, it is only a fit entrance for small vessels of a light draft of water, and even for small vessels it is dangerous to approach in bad weather.

[Coggeshall landed to find Napoleon's empire on the verge of collapse as the Allied Armies pressed in on France from all sides. Austrian and Russian troops were advancing on Paris and Wellington's British army was moving up from Spain. For the moment, however, Coggeshall was more concerned about his business difficulties with the Bordeaux merchants to whom his cargo was consigned. They flatly refused to handle it; although after much bickering they did advance him enough money to purchase a small cargo of wine and brandy. Coggeshall's plan was to send the Porter and her new cargo back to America, while he remained to look after the cotton. He knew that the sooner his ship set sail the better, for detachments of Wellington's forces were already reported close to Bordeaux.]

In the midst of all my trouble and confusion, I will devote a few moments to relate some of the peculiarities of this part of France. The large tract of country lying between Bayonne and Bordeaux is familiarly called the Landes. It is bounded on the west by the Bay of Biscay and extends about 25 leagues east into France. The face of the country is generally low, flat, sandy and barren. Its forests consist principally of pine or fir trees, and the land is generally miserably cultivated. The peasantry are wretchedly poor and mostly clothed in sheep skins. The Basque is the language of the country, and it is only the upper classes or educated people that speak French.

In the summer season the sands are extremely hot, and in the spring and fall months the country being low is often wet and muddy, which I suppose is the cause of so many of the country people—particularly the peasants and shepherds—walking on stilts, a foot or two above the ground, with a long balance pole to support them and regulate their movements.

I have seen them walking in the morning at a distance when the weather was a little foggy, when they absolutely appeared like immense giants walking over the tall grass and small trees. I used frequently to ask them why they preferred walking on stilts; their answer generally was to keep their feet dry, and remarking also that they could travel much faster and with more ease than with their feet on the ground. This region is very unlike any other part of France, and should a stranger visit the Landes without seeing any other part of the kingdom, he would naturally conclude that the French nation was only about half-civilized.

The pilot that took my vessel into port came off in a boat rowed (I liked to have said manned) by four females; and after the schooner came to anchor, I took one of my sailors with me and returned to the shore in the pilot's boat. We landed on a sand beach where the water was too shallow for the boat to come to the beach, when one of the women immediately jumped into the water, took the huge pilot on her back and carried him some distance to the dry land. Another female offered to carry me in the same way; to this I would not consent. The sailor, like myself, appeared ashamed to see a female carry a man on her back through the surf and instantly jumped out and took me on his back to the dry beach.

It is true, these women were coarse and rough, but still they were females and clad in petticoats, and it appeared wrong to my mind thus to degrade and debase the female character. All along the road from Lateste to Bordeaux I rarely saw a man at work in the fields. Nearly all the labor of cultivating the lands at that time was performed by females; now and then, it

is true, I saw an old man and perhaps a boy, but this did not often occur. All the men from sixteen to sixty were pressed into the military service. It was often a melancholy sight, when passing through the towns and villages, to see mere boys forced from their parents and taken to some military depot, there to be drilled for a few weeks and then sent to some of the numerous armies to be slaughtered like so many sheep and cattle.

Although at this period the Austrian and Russian armies were in the neighborhood of Paris, and Lord Wellington was marching at the head of his victorious army, overrunning the south of France, it was astonishing to see how little was known to the country people in this region about the military state of the kingdom. Perhaps not a man in a thousand knew that there was a Russian or an English soldier within a hundred leagues of France.

I recollect one day, passing through a small village, I stopped at a house to get some water. There I saw a poor woman wringing her hands and weeping ready to break her heart. I could not refrain from enquiring the cause of her grief, when she said: "Sir, they have just taken away my son to join the army, and I have already lost two of my children in the same way. Oh! I shall never see him again!"

Although at some hazard for my own safety, I voluntarily offered the poor woman all the consolation I could. I told her I was a stranger and had no right to interfere with the affairs of another nation, but at the same time, if she would keep quiet, I could assure her that there was no danger of losing her son; that the wars were nearly at an end, and that peace, in all human probability, woud be concluded in a few weeks, when her son would be restored to her again. At these words the poor creature was completely overjoyed. She blessed me a thousand times over, and when I mounted my horse and rode off, I was filled with indignation at what men call military glory; but at the next moment I felt self-reproved that I too commanded an armed vessel and was perhaps going out in a few days to distress the enemies of my country. Oh! then, how strange and inconsistent is poor shortsighted man, always condemning others, when often committing the same crime that he would fain fasten on his neighbor.

I soon saw that the French ladies and the working women are removed an immeasurable distance from each other, almost as much so as though they did not belong to the same species. I used often to pass a social evening at the hospitable mansion of my worthy consignee, Madame Campos, and frequently saw there assembled some fifteen or twenty young ladies and generally not more than three or four gentlemen, and these were military officers who had been wounded and disabled in the wars and were now here attached to the custom house. This was certainly a sad state of society in a national point of view, when there were no young men to marry the fair daughters of France.

[*As the British approached, Coggeshall hastened to Bordeaux to prevent the landing of the wine shipment at Lateste. He ordered it sent instead to the heavily fortified port of La Rochelle, which was not yet in danger. Then he made ready to sail—and got away just in time, for the British occupied Lateste the day after he left.*]

On my arrival at Lateste, I lost no time in preparing for sea. There was no other ship or vessel lying here, and no stone ballast. I was therefore compelled to take in sand ballast in my own boat and fill up our water casks. We had no biscuit on board and there was but one baker of any consequence in the whole town. I hastened to this important character and agreed to take all the bread he could make in two days, and thus by hurrying and driving I got ready for sea on the 11th of March. At the end of two days I called on the baker for my supply of bread, when to my great mortification and disappointment I could get only loaves enough to fill two bags, and this for a vessel bound to La Rochelle with a crew of thirty-five in number was certainly a very small allowance. It is true I had salt beef and pork enough on board, but no vegetables or rice.

On the 11th in the evening, by letters from Bordeaux, I learned that the day before, on the 10th, the town had surrendered by capitulation to a portion of Lord Wellington's army, that no person had been molested, and that perfect good order was observed throughout the city.

All this appeared very well with respect to Bordeaux, but still I was fearful that the English would come down and take Lateste before I could get to sea. The next day, March 12th, the wind was from the westward and the pilot would not take my vessel to sea. He said that it was impossible to get out, that there was too great a swell on the bar, etc. The next day, the 13th, the weather was clear and the wind fresh at N.N.E. In the morning I prevailed on the pilot to come on board. He told me that the tide would suit at five o'clock in the afternoon, and if there should not be too much sea on the bar at that hour, he would take the vessel out. Accordingly, at four o'clock I requested him to get under weigh and be ready to pass the bar at five. I now found he was unwilling to go out at all.

He said, "Captain, if we should succeed in getting out, it would be impossible to land me." I then offered him double pilotage, told him I was fearful the English would come down in the morning and make a prize of my vessel, and that I would treble his pilotage, and pledged him my honor that if I waited a week outside, I would land him in safety. At last my patience was exhausted, and I found the more I coaxed and strove to persuade him to go, the more obstinate he became. At length I said, "If you will not go to sea, pilot, just get the schooner under weigh, and go down below the fort and anchor there within the bar." To this proposition he consented.

While getting under weigh, I went below and put into my pocket a loaded pistol and again returned on deck. We soon got below the fort, and it was five o'clock, precisely the hour he had named as the most suitable to safe out over the bar. I then placed the pistol to his ear and told him to proceed to sea, or he was a dead man, and that if the schooner took the ground his life should pay the forfeit. The poor fellow was terribly frightened and said he would do his best; and thus, in less than fifteen minutes from the time we filled away, we were fairly over and outside of this dreadful bar. I then discharged the pistol and assured the pilot I would do him no harm, and that I would wait a week if it was necessary for good weather to land him in safety. He now appeared more tranquil and composed but could not refrain from talking occasionally of his poor wife and children and seemed to have a lurking fear that I would carry him to America.

I stood off and on during the night and in the morning, March 14th. The wind was light off shore from the eastward. As the sea was smooth I stood close in to the beach and got our boat ready to land the pilot. I gave him several letters to my friends and an order for a considerable sum over and above his regular pilotage, notwithstanding I had compelled him to take my vessel to sea. At eight o'clock in the morning, my second officer with four men took Mr. Pilot on shore. I gave the officer of the boat positive orders to back the boat, stern on to the shore, and let the pilot jump out whenever he could do so with safety. I took a spyglass and soon had the pleasure to see the man land and scamper up the beach.

The boat soon returned and was hoisted on board when we made sail and stood off in a N.W. direction. The wind was light from the eastward and the weather fine and clear. During the night we had not much wind and of course made but little progress. At daylight, March 15th, 1814, saw a large ship on our weather quarter. I soon made her out to be a frigate, distant about two miles. We were now in a very unpleasant position: early in the morning, with a frigate dead to windward. I manoeuvred for some ten or fifteen minutes in hopes of drawing him down to leeward so that I should be able to weather him on one tack or the other. (This was often done at the commencement of the war, with American schooners, for if the pilot boats could succeed in getting the enemy under their lee, they would laugh at their adversary.) This manoeuvre, however, did not succeed. He only kept off about 4 or 6 points, and I have no doubt he thought it impossible for me to elude his grasp. All this time I was losing ground, and the ship not more than two gun shots to windward.

I held a short consultation with my officers on the subject of attempting to get to windward, namely by receiving a broadside, or by running off to leeward. They all thought it best to ply the windward and receive his fire. I stated that we should have to pass him within pistol shot, and the probability was that he would shoot away some of our spars, in which case we should inevitably be captured. I knew the schooner sailed very fast off the wind, and I thought the chance of escape better to run to leeward. I accordingly gave orders to get the square sail and studding-sails all ready to run up at the same moment. The frigate, not dreaming of my running to leeward, was unprepared to chase off the wind, and I should think it was at least five minutes before he had a studding-sail set, so that I gained about a mile at the commencement of the chase.

The wind was light from the E.N.E. and the weather very fine. I ordered holes bored in all the water casks except four and the water pumped into buckets to wet the sails, also to throw overboard sand ballast to lighten the schooner. After this was done we began to draw away from the frigate, so that at noon I had gained eight or ten miles on the chase. At four in the afternoon he was nearly out of sight and appeared like a speck on the water.

We had now time to look into our own situation, when to my great regret, in lieu of leaving four casks of water, the carpenter in the confusion had only left two, and as the wind freshened I found the schooner so light that it was unsafe to haul upon the wind [to turn the ship to windward].

And now I will leave the seafaring men to judge of my unfortunate situation: Thus, wide off to sea in the Bay of Biscay, with a light vessel with scarcely ballast

enough to stand upon her bottom, with a crew of thirty-five men and only two casks of fresh water and a few loaves of soft bread.

The wind was light during the night, and towards morning it became almost calm. At daylight, to our unspeakable joy, we were in the midst of a small fleet of merchant ships. They had left England under convoy of a frigate and a sloop-of-war, and had separated in a gale of wind a few days before I fell in with them, and were now like a flock of sheep without a shepherd. This little fleet was bound to St. Sebastian, and many of them were loaded with provisions for the British Army. The first one I captured was a brig, principally laden with provision. After taking possession, I agreed with the captain that if he would assist me with his boats and men to transport his cargo from his vessel to

my schooner, I would let him go; otherwise I would take what I wanted and destroy his brig. Of course he was glad to make the best of a bad bargain, and thus, with the boats of both vessels, in two hours we had provisions enough for three months' cruise. His cabin was filled with bags of hard biscuit, and as this is considered the staff of life we took it first and then got a fine supply of butter, hams, cheese, potatoes, porter, etc., etc., and last, though not least, six casks of fresh water.

After this was done the captain asked me if I would make him a present of the brig and the residue of the cargo for his own private account, which I willingly agreed to in consideration of the assistance I had received from him and his men.

I showed him my commission from the Government of the United States, authorizing me to take, burn, sink, and destroy our common enemy, and satisfied him that he was a lawful prize to my vessel. I then gave him a certificate stating that though his brig was a lawful prize, I voluntarily gave her to him as a present. (This, of course, was only a piece of foolery, but it pleased the captain, and we parted good friends.)

This was on the 16th of March, the day after my escape from the British frigate.

I had now got as much water and provisions as I wanted, and made sail for a ship and two brigs, a mile or two off on our lee beam. Although the wind was very light, I soon took all three of them and made the same agreement with them as with the other captain, that if they would assist me with all their boats and help me to load my schooner with such part of their cargo as suited me, I would let them go; otherwise I would send them into port as prizes or destroy their vessels. This was a bitter pill, but they had the choice of two evils and of course complied with my request.

After having taken out a considerable quantity of merchandise, a fresh breeze sprang up from the S.W. and the weather became dark and rainy, which rendered it difficult to continue transporting any more goods from the prizes to our schooner.

At five o'clock in the afternoon a large ship hove in sight to windward. From aloft, with a spyglass, I clearly made her to be the same frigate that had chased me the day before. I recognized her from the circumstance of her having a white jib; all the sails were dark colored except this jib, and this was bleached. From this remarkable fact I was quite sure it was the same ship.

We of course cleared the decks and got ready for another trial of speed; but as my schooner was now in good trim, and night coming on, I had no doubt of dodging him in the dark. He came rapidly down within five or six miles of us when I ran near my prizes and ordered them all to hoist lanterns. Neither of them up to this time had seen the frigate; and thus while the lanterns showed their positions, I hauled off silently in the dark. Very soon after this I heard the frigate firing at his unfortunate countrymen, while we were partaking of an excellent supper at their expense.

The next day, March 17th, it was dark, rainy weather, with strong gales from the S.W. Saw nothing. Stood to the northward under easy sail, waiting for better weather to complete loading my little schooner with something valuable from another prize.

I would here remark that small guns, that is to say, 6- or 9-pounders, are of little or no use on board of small vessels, for if the sea is rough they cannot be used at all; in a word, I have found them of no service but rather in the way. My only dependance was on my 18-pounder, mounted amidships on a pivot. This gun I could use in almost any weather.

With this gun and forty small arms, I found no difficulty in capturing merchant ships. I selected ten of the largest and strongest of the men I had on board to work the center gun. One of these was a huge black man, about six feet six inches in height and large in proportion. To him I gave the command of the gun. Although so powerful a man, he was the best-natured fellow in the world and a general favorite with both officers and men.

March the 18th, still a continuation of bad weather with a strong gale from the westward. At 4 P.M. saw a frigate and a brig-of-war off my lee beam, distant about five miles. They made sail in chase, but under my three lower sails, namely mainsail, foresail and jib, I had no fear of them. I showed my ensign for a few moments and then plied to windward, taking short tacks; and in a few hours they gave up the chase, when I again pursued my course to the northward under easy sail. Next day, March 19th, the wind moderated, but still there was a very high sea and very unpleasant weather.

March 20th, moderate breezes from the westward and unpleasant weather. This day I came to the conclusion to land myself somewhere on the coast of France and to send my vessel home under the command of my first officer, Mr. Samuel Nichols; and on an examination of a chart of the coast, I concluded to run for l'Ile d'Yeu [an island lying below the mouth of the Loire River] and land there. Accordingly I shaped my course for the island, and without meeting with any incident worth relating made the land on the 23rd of March at four o'clock in the afternoon, and at six landed on the island in my own boat. It soon became dark and I was obliged to remain on shore with my boat's crew all night.

I took with me my clearance and other papers from Bordeaux, with sundry newspapers, and was well received by the governor and commissary of Marine.

March 24th at six o'clock in the morning, although the weather was thick and rainy and a strong breeze from the S.W., I sent my boat on board the schooner with a pilot, with orders to get the vessel into the roads near the town, which is situated on the N.E. end of the island. At two o'clock in the afternoon the schooner came directly off the town, close in with the fort, where with our own boat we took on board six casks of fresh water, some fresh provisions, and sundry small stores. I then obtained liberty from the public authorities to dispatch my vessel to the United States.

When I landed at l'Ile d'Yeu, I took with me as one of the boat's crew the large black man Philip, and I was astonished to see the curiosity expressed here at the sight of a Negro. He was followed at every step by a crowd of men, women and children, all desirous to see a black man; and I soon received a pressing message from the governor's lady to see him. I accordingly took Philip with me and repaired to the residence of the governor, where were assembled all the first ladies of the island. They had a great many questions to ask about him respecting the place of his birth, whether he was kind and good-natured, etc. When their curiosity was gratified, the fellow begged of me as a favor to be allowed to go on board, as he did not like to be exhibited as a show. This request I readily granted, telling the ladies and gentlemen that I had an Indian on board, and that I would send for him. The Indian came directly on shore, but to my surprise there appeared but little curiosity on the part of the inhabitants to see the savage.

When I came to reflect a little on the subject, I was not at all surprised at the novelty of seeing a black man. This island had been, as it were, shut out from the rest of the world for twenty-five or thirty years with little or no commerce or communication with other nations, and it is therefore highly probable that very few of its inhabitants had ever seen a Negro, and they were, of course, eager to behold one.

At five o'clock in the afternoon of March 24th, 1814, I repaired on board in a shore boat, and after writing a few hasty letters to my friends in the United States and making a short address to my officers and men, I resigned the command to my first lieutenant, Mr. Samuel Nichols, and returned on shore with a heavy heart at parting with my little band of faithful followers.

The schooner was soon out of sight as she stood round the south end of the islands, and here I should be doing injustice to the memory of these brave men did I not give my feeble testimony to their good conduct from the time we left Charleston until parting with them at l'Ile d'Yeu. I never saw one of them intoxicated in the slightest manner, nor did I ever see one of them ill-treat a prisoner or attempt to plunder the smallest article. In a word, from the first lieutenant to the smallest boy on board, they were faithful, good and true men, and to the best of my knowledge and belief were all born and bred in the United States.

[*Coggeshall proceeded to La Rochelle. While arranging for the transportation of his wine cargo on another letter-of-marque schooner, the* Ida, *he heard of the capture of Paris and the fall of Napoleon and his subsequent exile to Elba. The* Ida *and Coggeshall's uninsured property barely escaped capture. The schooner had to make a dash through a squadron of British men-of-war stationed at the mouth of the harbor; and though some of her rigging was shot away by cannon fire, she managed to outdistance her pursuers.*

When Coggeshall returned to Bordeaux, he was gratified to learn that most of his cotton had been sold. Next he journeyed to La Rochelle, Nantes, and finally, Paris, in an unsuccessful attempt to secure passage home. Nantes he found "the most moral town of its size in the kingdom"—but perhaps the reason was that "there appeared to be about three women to one man. . . ." Paris was, in his opinion, "astonishing," a city of "astounding sublimity." There Coggeshall purchased 5,000 francs worth of French silks, shawls, and silk stockings, which he sent to Bordeaux for shipment to the United States. Then he went sight-seeing.

Back in Bordeaux in September, he was informed that both the Porter *and the* Ida *had reached America safely. The* Porter *had captured several British prizes and arrived at Gloucester with considerable booty and several prisoners. Meanwhile Coggeshall decided not to take immediate passage home, and instead assumed command of the American schooner* Leo.]

The *Leo* was a fine Baltimore-built vessel of 320 tons burthen, sailed remarkably fast, and was in every respect a very superior vessel. This schooner was lying in L'Orient on the first of November, 1814, and then belonged to Thomas Lewis, Esq., an American gentleman residing in Bordeaux. She was purchased on the 2nd of November by an association of American gentlemen from Mr. Lewis and placed under my command. The commission of this vessel was endorsed over to me, and the whole transaction acknowledged and ratified by our Minister at Paris, the Honorable Wm. H. Crawford.

The object of the voyage was to make a little cruise and, if possible, take and man a few prizes, then proceed to Charleston for a cargo of cotton, and return from thence as soon as possible to France; and, as there was quite a number of American seamen in Bordeaux, Nantes, and L'Orient, supported by the Government of the United States through the consuls at the beforementioned ports, it was desirable to take home as many as the vessel could conveniently accommodate.

After the arrangement was made to perform the voyage, I took with me as first officer Mr. Pierre G. de Peyster, and left Bordeaux for L'Orient. On our way we stopped a day or two at Nantes, where I agreed with forty seamen and two petty officers to go with me in the *Leo* on our intended voyage. The arrangement with these men was made with the consent and sanction of our resident consul at that place.

Mr. Azor O. Lewis, a fine young gentleman, brother to the former owner of the *Leo*, was one of my prizemasters, and to him I committed the charge of bringing about forty seamen from Bordeaux to this place.

The residue of the officers and men were picked up at L'Orient, with the exception of four or five of my officers who came from Bordeaux and joined the vessel at this place.

Early in November we commenced fitting the *Leo* for sea. We found her hull in pretty good order, but her sails and rigging in rather a bad state. I, however, set everything in motion, namely sailmakers to repair the sails, block-makers, blacksmiths, etc., etc., while others were employed taking in ballast, filling up water casks, etc., in fine, hurrying on as fast as possible before we should be stopped. The English had so much interference with the new government of Louis XVIII that we, as Americans, felt extremely anxious to get out on the broad ocean as soon as possible, and therefore drove on almost night and day. After ballasting, we took on board 3 tons of bread, 30 barrels of beef, 15 ditto of pork and other stores to correspond; in short, I ordered stores enough for fifty days.

Our crew including the officers and mariners numbered about one hundred souls, and a better set of officers and men never left the port of L'Orient. But we were miserably armed. We had, when I first took the command of this schooner, one long brass 12-pounder and four small 4-pounders, with some fifty or sixty poor muskets. Those concerned in the vessel seemed to think we ought with so many men to capture prizes enough even without guns. With this miserable armament, while I was lying at anchor at the mouth of the harbor, waiting only for my papers from Paris, I was ordered by the public authorities to return to port and disarm the vessel. I was compelled to obey, and accordingly waited on the commanding officer and told him it was a cruel case that I should not be allowed arms enough to defend the vessel. He politely told me he was sorry, but that he must obey the orders of the government and that I must take out all the guns except one; and at the same time laughingly observed that one gun was enough to take a dozen English ships before I got to Charleston. I of course kept the long 12-pounder, and during the night we smuggled on board some twenty or thirty muskets. In this situation I left the port of L'Orient on the 8th of November, 1814, and stood out to sea in hopes of capturing a few prizes.

After getting to sea we rubbed up the muskets, and with this feeble armament steered for the chops of the British Channel. We soon found that when the weather was good and the sea smooth we could take merchantmen enough by boarding, but in rough weather our travelling 12-pounder was but a poor reliance and not to be depended upon, like the long counter gun that I had on board the *David Porter*. It is

true, my officers and men were always ready to board an enemy of three times our force, but in a high sea if one of these delicately Baltimore-built vessels should come in contact with a large, strong ship, the schooner would inevitably be crushed and knocked to pieces.

George
Coggeshall, Esq.

[*At this point in his narrative, Coggeshall introduces several weeks of entries from the log of the* Leo. *Entries of weather, latitude and longitude have been omitted here.*]

SUNDAY NOV. 13TH. At 6 A.M. saw a brig to windward. At seven she set English colors—gave her a gun when she struck her flag. She proved to be the English brig *Alexander*, Captain Crain, from Leghorn bound up the Channel. It now commenced blowing a strong breeze from the N.W. and soon there was a high sea running. Saw a large ship steering up the Channel; left the prize, made sail in chase of her. At 10 A.M. she set English colors and fired a gun. Had the weather been smooth, I think we could have carried her by boarding in fifteen minutes, or had I met her at sea I would have followed her until the weather was better and the sea smooth; but being now in the English Channel, with a high sea, it would have destroyed our schooner if she had come in contact with this wall-sided ship. He showed six long nines on each side. Thus after exchanging a few shot I hauled and let him go, and then returned to our prize. Fresh gales and cloudy weather.

MONDAY NOV. 14TH. At 2 P.M., the weather moderated, when I took out of the *Alexander* the captain, mate and crew, and put on board of her Mr. Turner as prize-master and seven men, with orders to proceed to a port in the United States.

TUESDAY NOV. 15TH. As it was now the middle of November and no prospect of much fine weather, and my schooner so badly armed, I concluded to leave this rough cruising ground and run to the southward in hopes of finding better weather.

WEDNESDAY NOV. 16TH. Saw a sail to the eastward, made sail in chase; at 9 A.M. boarded her. She proved to be the Spanish brig *Diligent*, Captain José Antonio de Bard, from Bilbao bound to London—put eight English prisoners on board of her with a tolerable supply of provisions, and let him proceed on his course. At 10 A.M. saw two sail to the westward when we made sail in chase.

THURSDAY NOV. 17TH.   Four sail in sight, light airs and fine weather. Made sail in chase of the nearest vessel at noon. The chase hove to and hoisted Spanish colors. When about to board this brig we discovered an English man-of-war very near, in full chase of us.

FRIDAY NOV. 18TH.   The man-of-war brig still in chase of us about two miles distant at 8 P.M. Passed near a brig standing to the eastward. Had not time to board her, as the man-of-war was still in chase. At midnight the wind became fresh from the W.S.W. with dark rainy weather. Took in all the light sails, and hauled close upon the wind to W.N.W. At 7 A.M. saw a small sail on our weather bow, made sail in chase. At ten, came up with the chase, found it was the English sloop *Brilliant*, Captain John Petrie, from Teneriffe bound to London with a cargo of wine.

SATURDAY NOV. 19TH.   At meridian took out of the prize twenty quarter-casks of wine, together with her sails, cables, rigging blocks, etc., and after removing the prisoners, scuttled her. At 1 P.M. she sank. Strong gales from the northward and rainy weather during the night.

SUNDAY NOV. 20TH.   At 7 A.M. saw a sail to windward, tacked ship to get the weather gage [that is, to get the advantage of the windward position]. At eleven, got her on our lee beam when we made her out to be an English brig-of-war of 16 guns. I commenced firing my long 12. At noon, after receiving about thirty or forty shot from this brig without any material damage, I hauled off. Some of his shot passed over us, some fell short; and only one of his shot hulled us; this shot passed through our bands amidships and lodged in the hold. I could outsail him with the greatest ease and if I had had a long, well-mounted centre gun, I could have annoyed him without receiving any injury by just keeping out of the reach of his cannonades.

MONDAY NOV. 21ST.   At meridian saw a sail bearing W.S.W. Made sail in chase. At 4 P.M., she being directly to leeward, I ran down to discover the character of the chase. I soon made her out to be a frigate. When within three miles distance I hoisted an English ensign. The frigate showed Portuguese colors and resorted to every stratagem in his power to decoy us down within the range of his shot. Finding I could outsail him with ease, I hauled down the English colors, set an American ensign, and hauled close upon the wind, and soon lost sight of him. During the night we had fresh gales at E.N.E. and squally weather.

TUESDAY NOV. 22ND.   At 7 A.M. made a small sail bearing S.S.W.; made sail in chase. We soon came up with and boarded the English schooner *Hannah*, Patrick Hodge, master, from Malaga bound to Dublin with a cargo of fruit. Took out the prisoners and a supply of fruit and then manned her and gave orders to the prize-master to make the best of his way to the United States of America. At 3 P.M. came up with and boarded a Danish galliot; at midnight put ten English prisoners on board of this galliot. I supplied them with provisions and a quarter-cask of wine and allowed him to proceed on his voyage. She was from Marseilles bound to Hamburg, with a cargo of wine and oil. At 8 A.M. saw a sail bearing N.N.E. Made sail in chase; at eleven boarded her. She proved to be a Swedish barque from St. Ubes bound to Stockholm.

WEDNESDAY NOV. 23RD.   At 1 P.M. wore ship to the S.E. in chase of a brig. She proved to be a Russian from Oporto bound to Hamburg, with a cargo of wine and fruit. At noon discovered two frigates to leeward. They both made sail in chase of us. I plied to windward, tacking every hour, and beat them with great ease, but as there were two of them I was not quite at ease until I had got out of their neighborhood.

THURSDAY NOV. 24TH.   Showers of rain and a high head sea running—the two frigates still in chase of us. At 5 P.M. the weathermost frigate was about ten or twelve miles distant to leeward. Finding I could beat them with so much ease, I reefed the sails and plied to windward. Towards morning the wind moderated and at daylight there was nothing in sight.

FRIDAY NOV. 25TH. At 3 P.M. discovered a sail bearing about S.E. Made sail and bore easy in chase. At half past three, made her out to be a frigate, when I hauled upon the wind. At four, she fired a gun and showed American colors. I set an American ensign for a few minutes, and then hauled it down and hoisted a large English ensign. He fired three or four shot, but finding they fell short, stopped firing and crowded all sail in chase. Night coming on, I soon lost sight of him. During the night we had fresh breezes and cloudy weather. At daylight there was nothing in sight; took in sail.

SATURDAY NOV. 26TH.   At 1 P.M. discovered a sail to windward bearing N.W. Made sail in chase, tacking every hour. At five made him out to be a ship standing upon the wind to the N.E. At half past nine o'clock, after getting on his weather quarter, ran up alongside, hailed him, and ordered him to heave to, which order was immediately obeyed. I sent my boat on board and found her to be the English ship *Speed*, burthen about 200 tons, Captain John Brown, from Palermo bound

77

to London with a cargo of brimstone, rags, mats, etc., etc. She mounted six guns with a crew of about twenty men. We kept company through the night.

SUNDAY NOV. 27TH. In the forenoon of this day removed the prisoners from the ship *Speed* and put Mr. Azor O. Lewis on board as prize-master, and a crew of ten men. I also took out his guns, powder, shot, and some fruit and then ordered Mr. Lewis to proceed to the United States. At 2 P.M. made sail and steered to the S.W. and at five lost sight of the prize.

THURSDAY DEC. 1ST. At 1 P.M. saw a ship on our weather quarter coming up with us very fast. I made sail upon the wind to the westward, to get to windward of the ship in order to ascertain her character.

It was then blowing a strong breeze from the N.N.W. and was somewhat squally with a head sea running. About half past two our schooner gave a sudden pitch, when to the astonishment of every person on board the foremast broke about one third part of the way below the head, and in a moment after it broke again, close to the deck. While in this situation I had the mortification to see the other ship pass within pistol shot, without being able to pursue her. I believe she was an English packet just out of Lisbon and bound for England, and I have not the smallest doubt, if it had not been for this dreadful accident, we should have captured her in less than one hour from the time we first saw her. At this time the packets transported large quantities of specie to England, and this ship would, in all human probability, have proved a rich prize to us.

[*Here Captain Coggeshall resumes his narrative.*]

I have no doubt the mast was defective and that it should have been renewed before leaving port; and to this circumstance I attribute all the misfortune attending the cruise. I cannot express the disappointment and mortification I now felt, not so much on my own account as on account of the loss incurred by the worthy gentlemen who planned and fitted out the expedition. Our only hope was to get into Lisbon or St. Ubes before daylight the next morning, and thus escape capture. We accordingly cleared away the wreck, rigged a jury-foremast and bore away for Lisbon. At 4 P.M., an hour after the accident occurred, we were going at the rate of seven knots, and had the breeze continued through the night we should have got into port by daylight next morning. But unfortunately the wind became light during the night and we made but little progress. At 5 A.M., daylight, made Cape Espartel and the Rock of Lisbon, when it became almost calm. We then commenced sweeping and towing with two boats ahead until 1 P.M., when a light air sprung up from the westward and I had strong hopes that we should be able to get into port or run the vessel on shore and destroy her, and thus escape capture.

At 2 P.M., being about four miles from the land, received a Lisbon pilot on board. At this time the ebb tide commenced running out the Tagus, when I had the mortification to see a frigate coming out with the first of the ebb, with a light air of wind from off land. Soon we were under her guns. She proved to be the *Granicus*, 38 guns, Captain W. F. Wise. We were all removed to the frigate and the schooner taken in tow for Gibraltar.

Two days after our capture, namely, the 3rd of December, we arrived at Gibraltar. All my officers and men were distributed and sent to England in different ships; myself and the first and second lieutenants were retained on board the *Granicus* to undergo an examination at the Admiralty Court at Gibraltar. The next day after our arrival the frigate left port for Tetuan Bay, Morocco, opposite Gibraltar, to water and paint the ship. We were taken on this little voyage, and had I not been a prisoner I should have enjoyed very much the novelty of this excursion, which occupied three or four days, after which time we again returned to Gibraltar.

Capt. Wise was a fine gentlemanly man and always treated me and my officers with great respect and kindness; we messed in the wardroom, and I had a stateroom to myself and was as comfortable and happy as I could be in the circumstances in which I was placed. I used to dine with Capt. W. almost daily; he frequently said to me, "Don't feel depressed by captivity, but strive to forget that you are a prisoner and imagine that you are only a passenger." He also invited my first lieutenant, Mr. de Peyster, occasionally to dine with him, and said he would endeavor to get us paroled and thus prevent our being sent to England.

We stated to him that we had voluntarily released more than thirty British prisoners, notwithstanding that the American government gave a bounty (to letters-of-marque and privateers) of one hundred dollars per head for British prisoners brought into the United States. These facts Capt. Wise represented to the governor and also added that the five English prisoners found on board the *Leo* said they had been very kindly treated, and he hoped his Excellency would release me and my two lieutenants upon our parole and let us return to the United States. The governor refused to comply with the kind request of Capt. Wise and said he had positive orders from the British government to send every American prisoner brought to that port to England.

When Capt. Wise informed us that he was unable to obtain our liberty on parole, he gave me a letter of introduction to a friend in England, requesting him to use his best interest to get myself and my first and second lieutenants released on parole and thus enable us to return forthwith to the United States.

Mr. Daly, an Irish gentleman, second lieutenant of the *Granicus* and a fine fellow, who was connected with several persons of distinction in England, also gave me a letter to a noble lady of great influence at Court. I regret I do not recollect her name but I clearly recollect the emphatic expression of the kindhearted and generous Daly when he handed me the letter to his noble friend. "Cause this letter to be presented," said he, "and upon it this lady will never allow you or your two friends to be sent to prison in England."

Mr. de Peyster was a high-spirited man, and when he learned that we could not obtain our liberty on parole, he became extremely vexed and excited and told the wardroom officers that, if it should ever please God to place him in command of a letter-of-marque or privateer during the war, he would never again release one English prisoner, but would have a place built in the vessel to confine them until he should arrive in the United States—that the bounty of $100 given by the United States government was nearly equal in value to an African slave, and therefore it became an object to carry them into port; but from motives of humanity we had released many of their countrymen and now they refused to parole three unfortunate men who were in their power. I said but little on the subject but from that moment resolved to make my escape the first opportunity.

The next day after this conversation, namely December 8th, Capt. Wise said, "Captain Coggeshall, it is necessary that you and your officers should go on shore to the Admiralty Office, there be examined with respect to the condemnation of your schooner, your late cruise, etc., and if you will pledge me your word and honor that you and your officers will not attempt to make your escape, I will permit you and the other two gentlemen to go on shore without a guard." I told him at once that I would pledge myself not to attempt in any way to make my escape and would also be answerable for Mr. de Peyster and Mr. Allen. This ready compliance on my part was only a ruse to gain an opportunity to reconnoitre the garrison or, in seamen's phrase, "to see how the land lay," in order to profit by the first chance to make my escape.

We accordingly went on shore without a guard and were conducted to the Admiralty Office. I was first examined and was asked a great many questions, the greatest part of which were printed; the answers were written down opposite the questions. It seemed to me to be more a matter of form than for any other purpose. By the by, many of the enquiries appeared to me very silly.

After they had finished with me they commenced with Mr. de Peyster, and after asking him a few questions the court of enquiry was adjourned until the next morning at ten o'clock; and after notifying us to be there precisely at the time appointed they dismissed us. We then took a stroll about the town for an hour or two, returned on board and reported ourselves to Capt. Wise. Up to this time not a shadow of suspicion was visible on the countenance of Capt. Wise or his officers that either of us would attempt to make our escape.

In the evening I consulted with Messrs. de Peyster and Allen on the subject of giving them the dodge the very first opportunity. I told them that if the Captain required my parole the next morning I would not give it, neither would I advise them to pledge their word and honor that they would not make their escape. I told them further that I was resolved to decamp the first moment I saw a favorable opportunity and would advise them to do the same, and not, from any motives of delicacy, to wait a moment for me.

The next morning when I dressed myself, I put all the money I had, say about 100 twenty-franc gold pieces, in a belt around my person, and some 15 or 20 Spanish dollars in my pocket with some other little relics and trifling keepsakes, and being thus prepared went to breakfast in the wardroom. About nine o'clock Capt. Wise sent for me into his cabin, when the following dialogue ensued: "Well, Coggeshall, I understand you and your officers are required at the Admiralty Office at ten o'clock, and, if you will pledge your honor as you did yesterday that you will neither of you attempt to make your escape, you may go ashore without a guard; otherwise I shall be obliged to send one with you." I watched his countenance closely for a moment to ascertain his real meaning and whether he was determined to adhere strictly to the words he had just uttered, and then replied, "Captain Wise, I am surprised that you should think it possible for anyone to make his escape from Gibraltar." He instantly saw I was sounding him, when he pleasantly but firmly said, "Come, come, it won't do. You must either pledge your word and honor that neither you nor your officers will attempt to make your escape, or I shall be compelled to send a guard with you." I felt a little touched, and promptly replied, "You had better send a guard, sir."

Accordingly he ordered the 3rd lieutenant to take a sergeant and four marines with him and conduct us to the Admiralty Office to finish our examination.

At the hour appointed they commenced where they had left off the day before with Mr. de Peyster. I was sitting in the courtroom and Mr. Allen standing at the door, when he beckoned to me. I instantly went to the door and found the lieutenant had left his post and was not in sight. I then asked the sergeant whether he would go with us a short distance up the street to take a glass of wine. He readily complied with my request, leaving the marines at the door to watch Mr. de Peyster, and walked along respectfully a few paces behind us up the street.

We soon came to a wine shop on a corner with a door opening on each street. While the soldier was standing at the door, Mr. A. and myself entered and called for a glass of wine. I drank a glass in haste but unfortunately had no small change, and this circum-

stance alone prevented my worthy friend from going with me. I hastily told him I would cross the little square in front, turn the first corner, and there wait for him to join me. I then slipped out of the shop, passed quickly over the little park, and turned the corner agreed upon, without being seen by the sergeant while he was watching at the opposite door. I waited some minutes on the corner for Mr. Allen and was sadly disappointed that he did not make his appearance.

I had now fairly committed myself and found I had not a moment to spare. I therefore walked with a quick step towards the Land-Port-Gate, not the one leading to the peninsula, but the gate situated at the N.W. extremity of the town. My dress was a blue coat, black stock, and black cockade with an eagle in the centre. The eagle I took care to remove and then it was *tout à fait* an English cockade, and I had altogether very much the appearance of an English naval officer. I said to myself when approaching the guard at the gate, now is the critical moment, and the most perfect composure and consummate impudence is necessary to a successful result. I therefore gave a severe look at the sentinel when he returned me a respectful salute, and I was, in another moment, without the walls of the garrison.

I walked deliberately down on the mole or quay, where I was accosted by a great number of watermen, offering to convey me on board of my vessel. I employed one, and after getting off in the bay, he said, "Captain, which is your vessel?" Here again I was at a loss to decide on an answer, but after gazing for a few moments on the different ships and the flags of different nations, my eye caught sight of a galliot with a Norwegian ensign flying, and I said to myself, "The Norwegians are a virtuous, honest people and I am not afraid to trust them." I had been in Sweden and understood the character of these hardy, honest-hearted sons of the North; and thus, after a moment's hesitation, I replied to the boatman, "That is my vessel," pointing to the friendly galliot, and we were soon alongside.

I jumped on board and enquired for the captain, who soon made his appearance. I told him I had something to communicate to him. He told me to follow him into the cabin. I immediately asked him whether he was willing to befriend a man in distress. He said, "Tell me your story, and I will try to serve you." I frankly told him I was the captain of the American letter-of-marque schooner lately sent into port by the frigate *Granicus,* and that I had made my escape from the garrison and desired to get over to Algeciras as soon as possible, that I had money enough, but still I wanted his friendship, confidence and protection.

The good old gentleman had scarcely waited to hear my story to the end, before he grasped me by the hand and said in a kind, feeling manner, "I will be your friend, I will protect you. I was once a prisoner in England, I know what it is to be a prisoner. Rest assured, my dear sir, I will do all I can to assist you." I offered him a dollar to pay and discharge the boatman and remained myself below in the cabin. He said, "Put up your money, I have small change and will pay him what is just and right."

After dispatching the boatman he returned below and said, "Now take off your coat—put on this large pea-jacket and fur cap." In this costume, and with a large pipe in my mouth, I was in less than two minutes transformed into a regular Norwegian. Returning again on deck, I asked my good friend the captain whether I could rely on his mate and sailors not to betray me. He said, "They are honest and perfectly trustworthy, and you need be under no apprehension on their account." We took a social dinner together, when he observed, "I will now go on shore for an hour or two and hear all I can about your escape, and will come back early in the evening and relate to you all I can collect."

In the evening the old captain returned pleased and delighted. He said he never saw such a hubbub as there was about town: that the whole garrison seemed to be on the lookout—that the town major with the military and civil police were searching every hole and corner in Gibraltar for the captain of the American privateer—that both of my officers were put in confinement, and that the lieutenant of the frigate who had the charge of us had been arrested; in short, there was the devil to pay, all because the captain of the privateer could not be found.

The next morning I stated to my worthy friend how extremely anxious I was to go over to Algeciras, and how mortified I should be to be taken again on board the *Granicus*. He answered, "Leave that to me—I am well acquainted with a gang of smugglers that belong to Algeciras and often sell them gin, tobacco and other articles of trade. They will be here on board of my galliot at nine o'clock this evening and will probably start for Algeciras about midnight after they have made all their purchases. When they come, I will arrange with them to take you as a passenger."

About nine o'clock that evening a long, fast-rowing boat came silently alongside filled with men, and certainly a more desperate, villainous looking set were never seen. Their leader and several of his men came on board the galliot, and, after having purchased several articles and taken a glass of gin all round, the old captain enquired of the patroon of the boat what hour he intended to start for Algeciras, and said that the reason of his asking the question was that his brother wanted to go to that place for a few days upon business, and wished to engage a passage for him, and that he should be glad if his brother could lodge for a few days with his family. He answered that he should return again about midnight and would willingly take his brother, and that if he would put up with common rough fare, he was welcome to stay at his house as long as he pleased.

I accordingly got ready my little bundle which consisted of a few little things such as a shirt or two (for I did not forget to wear three at the time I left the *Granicus*) stowed away in my hat, and then tied up in a handkerchief, and this constituted the whole of my wardrobe. I agreed with my friend the Norwegian to leave the cap and pea-jacket with the American consul at Algeciras, to be returned to him by some safe conveyance in the course of a few days. Agreeable to promise, the boat came on board precisely at twelve o'clock, and after my friend the captain had again cautioned the patroon of the boat to take good care of his brother, we started.

The water in the bay was smooth, though the night was dark and favorable to the safe prosecution of the passage across the bay. The distance is about 8 or 10 miles from Gibraltar, and after rowing about two hours we arrived near the harbor, when we showed a light in a lantern for a minute or two and then covered it with a jacket. This signal was repeated two or three times until it was answered in the same way from the shore. We approached the port cautiously and landed in silence. The patroon took me by the arm and led me through many a dark winding passage.

On our way we passed by several sentinels and were frequently hailed with the shrill sound of *"Quien viva?"* To these salutations some friendly answer returned, and thus everything passed smoothly on, until at length we arrived at the humble dwelling of the smugglers.

In Spain the *contrabandistas* are a desperate class of men and often spread dread and fear through a wide region of the country. In many instances, they are so numerous and strong that they often put the whole power of the government at defiance. The gang that brought me to Algeciras was about twenty in number, all armed to the teeth with long knives, pistols, swords, etc., and had no doubt made their arrangements during the day with the officers and sentinels that were to mount guard that night. They, of course, made them a compensation in some way or other, in order that they should meet with nothing to interfere with or obstruct their nocturnal enterprises.

Early in life I had made several voyages to Spain and its colonies in America and had thus acquired a pretty good knowledge of the Spanish character. I had also picked up enough of the language to enable me to make my way among them without difficulty.

There is something about the Spaniard that immediately inspires confidence, so much so, that although surrounded by this desperate and daring gang of smugglers, I had not the smallest fear for my safety. It was now near three o'clock in the morning when we entered the small, low cabin of the patroon. The interior consisted of one tolerable size room with a mat hung up to serve as a partition to separate the different members of the family, which consisted of the patroon, Antonio, his wife and two children.

With this family I was soon placed upon the most friendly and intimate footing: a straw bed was prepared for me behind the neat screen. Before saying good night, Antonio told me he should leave the house very early in the morning to look after his boat and smuggled goods, and should not return until noon next day. He said his wife and little daughter would provide breakfast for me and would purchase whatever I wished at any time. After these preliminaries were settled, we all said "*Buenos noches*" and dropped asleep. About seven o'clock the next morning I furnished the smuggler's wife with money to purchase bread, butter, eggs and coffee; and when breakfast was prepared we all ate our social meal together, that is to say, the mother, the two children and myself. I then took a stroll about the town of Algeciras in my Norwegian costume and silently observed what was going on, without conversing with any person; and when I entered a coffee house, I took a newspaper and, as I said nothing, no one appeared to notice me. I had broken the quarantine laws and therefore deemed it prudent to keep on my disguise for a few days and continue to live in perfect seclusion.

Antonio was absent almost all the time during the three days I remained in his family. I furnished money for every meal, and the good Maria purchased and prepared our frugal meals. When I returned from a stroll about the town I always took care to provide cakes and bonbons for the children, so that we soon became good friends

and all lived very happily together and upon terms of the most perfect equality.

After remaining here for a period of three days, I began to tire of this mode of life and was now determined to ascertain how I should proceed to get to Cadiz, where I knew I should find friends and be farther removed from the mortifying scenes through which I had so lately passed. Accordingly, on the morning of the fourth day after my landing at Algeciras, I repaired to a café and enquired of one of the servants whether there was an American consul residing in the city. The boy seemed intelligent and instantly replied that Don Horatio Sprague, the former consul at Gibraltar, was residing here, and that he was "*un hombre de bien*." I asked for his address when he called a boy to show me the house, so that in fifteen minutes after I was knocking on Mr. Sprague's door.

He was of course surprised to see a man of my appearance walk boldly into his parlor. I soon however explained that I was not exactly what I appeared to be, that I was an American in distress, and throwing off my great fur cap and pea-jacket, looked somewhat more like an American. I told my story and was re-

ceived and treated like a brother. He was just going to take breakfast and said, "You will breakfast with us, and then I will send my nephew, Mr. Leach, with you for your bundle, and you will then return and take up your abode with me during your stay at Algeciras."

After a social breakfast, I doffed my cap and pea-jacket, and being supplied with a hat and other articles of dress to correspond, Mr. Leach kindly accompanied me to the humble dwelling of Maria. To my great surprise, on entering the cabin, the poor woman was very distant, curtseying with profound respect, and appeared altogether like another person. The children were shy and appeared to avoid me. At first, I felt hurt at the alteration, but a moment's reflection convinced me that the scene was quite natural, and I loved them not the less for their distant behavior. While in my disguise they looked upon me as one of the family, and now that the scene was changed, they looked upon me in quite another light; and I felt for a moment that the artificial rules of society were chilling to a generous heart. Maria told Mr. Leach that she always thought I was a gentleman, and that she was quite happy to serve me. After making the family suitable presents I took my leave, promising that they should frequently see me while I remained in Algeciras, which promise I took care rigidly to fulfill.

I had now entered as it were upon a new life, was quite at home with one of the best of men whose greatest pleasure has ever been to make others happy. His excellent nephew, William Leach, Esq., was also a fine young gentleman, and as we were all Americans together the most perfect confidence reigned throughout this delightful family.

During my stay here I was exceedingly amused with a little incident that occurred while at dinner at Mr. Sprague's table. A young English friend came over one Sunday to dine with Mr. S. During the dinner, Mr. S. asked the young man what was said in Gibraltar about the captain of the American letter-of-marque making his escape from the garrison. He said that it caused a great deal of excitement and speculation. Some said the lieutenant that had charge of him was very culpable and even insinuated that there must have been bribery connected with the business, that it was altogether a very strange affair that a man should be able in open daylight to make his escape from Gibraltar; and thus, after answering many questions on the subject, he wound up by saying that the captain must be a very clever man, and for his part he wished him God-speed. The young man had not the least suspicion that I was an American or had any connection with the business. During the conversation, whenever I caught the eye of Mr. Leach, it was with the greatest

difficulty I could command my countenance. Everything, however, passed off very well, and we often joked on the subject of the honest simplicity of their young English friend.

I remained from day to day at Algeciras, anxiously waiting to hear from my two lieutenants, Messrs. de Peyster and Allen, in hopes by some means they would be able to make their escape and not be sent prisoners to England.

I used frequently to ride in the country with Mr. Sprague in the evening, and we frequently made up an agreeable whist party, and among other social enjoyments my young friend Leach introduced me to two or three respectable and very agreeable Spanish families. In these families I spent many pleasant evenings in the society of several young ladies and gentlemen, and had my officers and crew been at liberty, I should have been quite contented and happy. At length, after waiting here about ten days, I learned with pain and sincere regret that all my officers and men had been sent prisoners to England, and I now seriously began to think of leaving this place for Cadiz.

There are but two ways of travelling with safety in Spain: one way is genteel and expensive, namely, with a strong guard of soldiers. The other is in simple disguise, so that no robber can feel any interest in molesting you on the road. This mode I determined to adopt.

After remaining in Algeciras about a fortnight, I hired a mule and a guide (through Mr. Sprague) to Cadiz. My kind friends furnished me with provisions and stores for a journey of two days. I procured a dress such as the peasants wear in this part of Andalusia, and thus equipped, on the morning of the 25th of December, 1814, I bade adieu to my two excellent friends from whom I had received so many disinterested favors.

After leaving the town, we travelled about a league on a tolerable smooth road and then turned off into a winding footpath, myself on the mule, and my guide, a merry fellow, trudging along on foot, sometimes by my side, sometimes a few yards ahead, and when we came to a smooth path I allowed him to ride on the mule behind me. The distance from Algeciras to Cadiz is about 40 miles, and I soon found we had a very intricate and difficult journey to perform. The whole country had a most wild and desolate appearance. In fact it seemed to me that there could have been little or no change in this part of Spain for the last five or six centuries. There were no public roads, a very thin and scattered population, and these living in a wretched state of poverty. Sometimes we travelled through deep and dark ravines, overgrown with trees and bushes; and after passing through a deep and gloomy dell, where we lost sight of the sun at times for a space of half an hour, we would then commence ascending a high mountain. We generally found a time-worn footpath running in a zigzag direction up these dreary mountains. This mode of ascending would, in seaman's phrase, be called "beating up." It certainly is a slow and fatiguing mode of ascent, but the traveller is richly rewarded for all his toil when once on the top of one of these stupendous mountains. Here he has a splendid view of the Strait of Gibraltar and the broad Atlantic, on the south and east, while the wild and unbroken scenery of the surrounding country is truly magnificent.

I will here remark that the people of the United States can scarcely believe that an old country like Spain should be in such a wretched condition as I found this part of the country, without roads, the land generally uncultivated, no hotels or taverns to accommodate strangers, and infested with robbers and banditti. Even in the vicinity of cities and towns, there is no safety in travelling without a military guard. This is certainly a dark and gloomy picture of poor Spain, once so great and powerful, now distracted by factions and civil war, divested of the greatest part of her once rich colonies, her government weak, without money and without credit.

If asked what is the cause of her degradation and dreadful downfall, I answer, there are many, but the principal ones are ignorance, idleness, superstition, priestcraft and bad government. I here involuntarily exclaim, oh! happy America! how glorious art thou among the nations of the earth! Long may an all-wise Being shower His benign blessings upon thee!

Postscript: Coggeshall arrived safely in Cadiz after an uneventful trip. Two months later he sailed to Lisbon and there embarked for America on a Portuguese brig. "On the 9th of May [1815]," he wrote, "we got a Sandy Hook pilot on board and the same day arrived in New York, and I was rejoiced to land once more in the United States after an absence of sixteen months and twenty-one days." During that time he could boast of the capture of nine British prize ships. To be sure, the Leo *had been lost, but the ship itself was to blame. The warrior merchant Coggeshall had also made a small but respectable profit, for he had not forgotten what Calvin Coolidge would remind the nation of over a hundred years later—that the business of America is business.*

After a long, arduous, and reasonably successful career at sea, Coggeshall retired in 1841. Always an avid reader and an indefatigable journal-keeper, he turned to writing in his declining years. Among his published works are Voyages to Various Parts of the World *and* History of American Privateers. *Coggeshall died in Milford on August 6, 1861, at the age of 77.*

READING, WRITING, AND HISTORY

By BRUCE CATTON

The Romantic Outlook

It may be that we would all be better off if we could rid history of some of the romantic haze which keeps blurring the outlines. This (it is only fair to add) is a responsibility of the citizen at large as well as of the historian. The romance is there, all right, and there is no way to avoid seeing it; the trick is to keep that fact from distorting our scale of values.

The romantic outlook does no particular harm if it is confined to the past. The trouble is that it won't stay there. It gets into the present as well, and then it represents a flight from reality. It embodies an attitude toward life—an attempt to perpetuate an impossible dream-image of bygone times—which makes it impossible to cope with today's problems. When that happens the future is apt to become rather difficult.

As a case in point, consider the American Civil War.

Whatever values we may see when we look back on that war—and both the romanticist and the cold realist can find plenty to look at—what stays with one the longest is the realization that the whole tragic business represented a national inability to face up to the future. The future was arriving, in the 1860's—what we live with now was struggling then to be born—and the need to study it and make the inevitable adjustments was simply too much for everybody. The war was an attempt to escape, with men on both sides imagining that they would preserve (each section in its own way) a cherished version of the past. The romantic outlook could hardly be followed with greater te-

nacity, nor could it easily lead to a greater disaster.

The one Civil War figure who, more than any other, draws the attention of the romanticist is that famous leader of Robert E. Lee's cavalry, Major General James Ewell Brown Stuart. You have to adopt the romantic outlook in looking at Stuart because there is no other way to see him. He wore a gray cape lined with scarlet, he kept a plume in his hat, when he rode off on some perilous expedition he went gaily, with a banjo player twanging a lively tune and the whole staff, as likely as not, joining in song; and he could posture for his own eyes and the eyes of posterity at the same time that he was most efficiently leading a hard-hitting group of fighting horsemen. He is presented now in a good new biography by Burke Davis—*Jeb Stuart, the Last Cavalier*—which is very much worth reading.

Mr. Davis has the right title. Stuart was the last cavalier. The Civil War was the last war in which he could have operated; indeed—and this is perhaps the point of the whole business—he was just slightly obsolete even for the Civil War, although neither he nor the men who fought against him ever suspected it. He saw war as a matter of gallantry and the heroic gesture, and it had got past that. He comes down to us as a streak of bright color in a darkening landscape, and he was never able to see why things were clouding up so badly because he was out of touch with the realities of his day. The ultimate realities of life and death he knew very well, and they never scared him. When his time came to die he played his part perfectly; carried off the field at Yellow Tavern with a mortal wound (an uncommonly painful one, to boot) he could call out to his troopers to go on back and give the Yankees another round, adding grimly and quite truthfully: "I would rather die than be whipped!" But of the larger reality in which his life was cast Stuart apparently understood very little.

Which is to say that he was pure act; a man of enormous gusto, who was the last cavalier without suspecting that something more than a cavalier was needed. Long before he died his deeds had become legendary. He twice rode completely around McClellan's army, he deftly screened Lee's army from prying Yankee cavalry, and when he took his men into battle—which he did with enormous enthusiasm whenever the chance offered—he was usually up in the front line himself, doing his own personal cutting and thrusting. As a soldier he was wholly admirable; the only trouble was that he was fighting in the wrong war.

War had ceased to be a romantic adventure. Traditionally, it was something that a nation might do with its left hand, carrying it on until the other side concluded that everybody might be better off if the fighting stopped, at which point some sort of accommodation would be reached. By the 1860's war had taken on the two terrible characteristics of modern war; neither participant could afford to stop anywhere short of complete, unconditional victory, and each discovered as it fought that to win a modern war a nation has to use every resource it has, from the farmer's corncrib or the village machine shop on up to the last full measure of the citizen's devotion. The converse of this, of

---

Jeb Stuart, the Last Cavalier, by Burke Davis. Rinehart & Co. 480 pp. $6.

---

course, is that you have to destroy every resource your enemy has, no matter where that leads you. It has led us in these later years considerably beyond our depth; even in the Civil War it led people farther than anyone intended to go, farther than anyone was ready to understand.

It had led them, for instance, beyond the point at which war could be won by cut-and-thrust cavalrymen pounding along in the grand manner. Stuart's own romantic concept tripped him at Gettysburg, where he saw the glamour of a bold cavalry raid so much more clearly than he saw what he was supposed to do to help Lee. In the end, it is possible to argue that roughhewn Bedford Forrest, who would not have recognized a romantic notion if it had hit him in the eye, had a better understanding of what mounted troops ought to be doing than Stuart had. The Stuart story is colorful and inspirational, but at bottom it is the tragic

story of a man who came on the scene in the wrong era. That tragedy he shared with his entire generation.

Sea Raider

What was true on the land was also true on the water. The sea raid was like the cavalry raid. It was bold, eye-filling, inspiring, and in the grand tradition, and it could be done (given the right leader) with the materials at hand. But it did not—in the nature of things, it could not—lead to final victory. Undying legends could be erected on the exploits of a Confederate cruiser like *Alabama,* which flitted across the seven seas like a destroying wraith, a great ship under a great captain; but to destroy the Northerners' ability to go on with the war something quite different was needed—something like the makeshift improvisations that produced the ironclads *Merrimac* and *Tennessee,* which could hit the Yankees where they really lived.

It was *Alabama* that got the attention, however; *Alabama,* and her famous skipper, Raphael Semmes, who was the Confederate Navy's exact counterpart of Jeb Stuart. Like Stuart, Semmes was brave, competent, and effective, with a flair for that little something extra which the born leader of men has to have. He had every qualification he needed for his job, but the job itself was a fragment from the earlier wars, aimed at the sort of thing that might have brought victory in the old days but that could not possibly do it in the Civil War.

Semmes gets the full treatment in Edward Boykin's new book, *Ghost Ship of the Confederacy,* and a fine tale it is. Semmes may have been the most accomplished commerce destroyer who ever lived. Putting to sea in 1861 in a rickety teakettle of a converted merchantman hastily fitted out as a cruiser and given the name *Sumter,* he took eighteen prizes, drove the Federal Navy almost frantic, and wound up at last at Gibraltar, with his ship almost ready to fall apart. Leaving it there, he went to England, took over the British-built and British-manned *Alabama,* and went off on one of the great sea raids of all time. In 22 months he roamed the Atlantic and Indian oceans and took 69 prizes. The American flag was all but driven from the sea, and American ship owners, hit squarely in the pocketbook, cried in anguish that this Semmes was a pirate who wanted hanging. All in all, Captain Semmes did his foes a good deal of harm.

But if Yankee commerce was extremely vulnerable to a daring sea raider, the Yankee nation itself was not. The war had taken on a new dimension, and it could never be won by commerce raiding any more than it could be won by heroic cavalry raids. It could be won, finally, only when one contestant or the other had been made utterly incapable of going on with the fight, and in the grim totality of that kind of war the commerce destroyer did not pack enough weight.

Ghost Ship of the Confederacy, by Edward Boykin. Funk & Wagnalls. 404 pp. $4.95.

Semmes cost the American shipping community enormous sums, but the American economy as a whole kept growing stronger. Semmes did perfectly what he was supposed to do; it was the job itself that failed to measure up.

Like Stuart, Semmes played his part with an air, right to the end. Late in the spring of 1864, U.S.S. *Kearsarge* caught up with him while he was at anchor in Cherbourg Harbor. Semmes served formal notice on Captain Winslow, of *Kearsarge,* that he would go outside and fight just as soon as he finished a few shore-side arrangements, and Winslow quietly accepted the challenge. (The whole business reminds one of two lace-cuffed duelists arranging for a meeting under the trees at tomorrow's dawn.) Presently the two warships left the harbor, almost in company, steamed carefully out past the limit of French territorial waters, and then squared off and began to fight.

The fight went quickly wrong, for Semmes. His fuses and powder were defective, and Winslow's gun crews were much better marksmen than his. In little more than an hour *Alabama* was a sinking wreck. She went down, *Kearsarge* picked up some of the crew, Semmes and others were rescued by a British yacht—which promptly took them off to England, out of the reach of vengeful Yankees—and the great story was over.

So it was a great story—and nothing more. Like Stuart, Semmes was on a dead-end street. Glamorous cavalry and glamorous sea raider alike came out of the romantic idea of war; that is, they were born of a national viewpoint by which the present had to resemble the past. They could do magnificent things, leaving a bright streak of color on the land and the sea—and, in the end, the war would go on about as it would have done if these things had not been.

Realist's War

Perhaps General William Tecumseh Sherman had caught the idea. It might be going too far to say that he had thought the thing through, but something in him seemed to respond instinctively to the changed condition. He fitted in, where Stuart and Semmes did not. He was no man for the knightly gesture or the grand flourish that both of these men understood so well, but he knew precisely what to do when he came across the enemy's corncribs and machine shops and he did it without a qualm. What he did finally won the war, but it was not very pretty.

For a firsthand glimpse of it you might read *When the World Ended,* which is the diary of a seventeen-year-old girl who lived in Columbia, South Carolina, edited by Earl Schenck Miers and brought forward here as an illustration of the unhappy fact that war in the modern world embodies things which the romantic outlook overlooks.

Emma LeConte lived in Columbia just when Sherman's destroying army came marching into the place and turned the greater part of the city into rubble. Her diary tells what she saw, felt, and experienced. It is hysterical, unbalanced, bitterly biased—and true; which is to say that she tells us, from an extremely partisan viewpoint, what the people of South Carolina felt when the destroying horde finally descended upon them.

The fact that there is in this book a strong touch of that departure from reality which was experienced by so many ardent Confederates (to say nothing of a great many ardent Northerners as well) simply gives it added point. The war which began as an inspiring

---

When the World Ended; the Diary of Emma Le-Conte, edited by Earl Schenck Miers. Oxford University Press. 124 pp. $4.

---

and romantic thing got very grim, finally, and there is little of romantic inspiration in the story of Sherman's march across the Carolinas. Whatever of final gain for all the nation there may have been in the Civil War was not readily visible to a teen-ager in Columbia in the early weeks of 1865, and you cannot expect to find a recognition of it in this diary.

What you do find is the undeniable fact that Sherman's men did a great deal to earn the hatred which the people of South Carolina felt for them. They went across the state like (and it was an expression the men themselves fancied) the wrath of God. They had an animus, and they felt justified in expressing it. They were imperfectly disciplined, and among them there were a good many out-and-out rowdies, and they looted and burned without giving the matter a second thought. They rationalized it, later (whenever it occurred to them that rationalization might be needed), by remarking that the war had to be won and that anyhow South Carolina had started it, but it does no one any harm to see how the whole business looked to a girl who was on the receiving end of it.

The war *had* to be won: perhaps that is the sentence

that does the damage. In the old days there were limits; there were things you did not have to endure and things you did not have to do, and when the pinch came you could simply stop fighting and work out some sort of settlement. War has got beyond that now because the stakes are always immeasurable. Neither the North nor the South imagined that the war they began at Fort Sumter was going to be like that. Their belief that it was going to be of the old, limited kind was basically a romantic belief. The present was going to be like the past. Unfortunately, it was not in the least like it, and the blackened ruins of burned Columbia lay on the sky line in testimony of it.

Young Innocents

Bear in mind that this romantic viewpoint was by no means confined to the South. It was all but universal, and you can see it in the North as well as in Dixie. It is eminently visible in the history of any of the hundreds of volunteer regiments which wore the Federal blue; very strikingly so, at this moment, in an excellent new book, *The Twentieth Maine*, by John J. Pullen, which tells how a typical regiment was organized, what it did, and how its members reacted to the whole affair.

The Twentieth Maine was formed in 1862, mostly from small towns and backwoods areas in the state of Maine, and its recruits came to camp with the quaintest notions of what they were getting into. Discipline, in the beginning, was entirely nonexistent. The regiment's first colonel was a starchy West Pointer named Adelbert Ames, and what he saw when he got to camp horrified him beyond measure. Instead of saluting, lanky privates leaning against trees would casually remark, "How d'ye do, Colonel?" when he came along. At guard mount, the officer of the day might show up in a cutaway coat and a silk hat—formal enough, if not exactly military—and when orders were issued the men would hold impromptu town meetings to discuss them and determine whether they ought to be obeyed. After his first inspection, Colonel Ames exploded wrathfully: "This is a hell of a regiment!" Then he set to work to put it into shape.

He succeeded admirably, and the Twentieth Maine became one of the most solid of Union combat outfits. It learned to salute and to obey orders and to appear on parade in proper uniform, and in the end it did a horrifying amount of very hard fighting—it was one of several Union regiments which claimed to have saved the day at Gettysburg, which was an occasion where the day needed saving repeatedly—and it served to the end of the war, counting among its veterans, finally, three winners of the Congressional Medal of Honor.

All in all, this regiment was typical; typical chiefly in that its members went off to war (like the nation that bore them) without the faintest conception of what was going to happen. They thought of war in the beginning as a sort of joint venture carried on by youthful heroes, who would picturesquely do fine things with great daring for flag and country; on their own level, they had the Jeb Stuart idea. They were caught up in something they did not understand, and what they would actually do was not at all like what they had bargained for when they enlisted.

They were, in short, a collection of young innocents, in which they precisely resembled most of their fellow countrymen, North and South alike. But what innocent people can do when they wage modern war can be rather terrifying, and in a small way Miss Emma LeConte has some testimony on the matter.

Sherman's army which wrecked Columbia was made up of regiments exactly like this one. Somewhere along the way its men were taught that they would win the war by wrecking the Southern economy, which meant by destroying all of the means that kept the economy functioning. Do this with a poorly disciplined, inadequately indoctrinated army and you are apt to loose horror on the land. Between burning a farmer's barn and killing his livestock (necessary, if

---

The Twentieth Maine, by John J. Pullen. The J. B. Lippincott Company. 352 pp. $5.

---

total war is to be won) and destroying a city that has already been captured, there is a dividing line which is all too easily crossed if the men who come up to it are disillusioned romantics who have learned that anything goes.

This is not simply a matter for solemn head-shaking by one reading the story of the Civil War in the quiet of his study. The problem is still with us, raised by now to quadruple strength. Modern war, just dawning in the 1860's, has come to its high noon—and we still have not thought our way through it. Subconsciously, we still approach the idea of war with the feeling that war can be limited and kept within some sort of restraints, which does not seem to be the case. Our ability to make war has developed much faster than our thinking about war. We still have the Jeb Stuart viewpoint, but in actions we tend to follow the pattern set by Sherman's bummers.

The historian Carl L. Becker once remarked that America is a society which needs to re-examine its theory of itself. Somehow we have let that re-examination lag. A good place to begin might be with a study of the gap between theory and reality in the Civil War.

worry they had to put into it. He asked if white men enjoyed working as much as the Utes enjoyed their lordly leisure of hunting and fishing and riding their ponies about their Colorado estate.

That fall agent Meeker discovered a perfect site for his model Ute farm at Powell Park a dozen miles down White River. He was sure of its value because the Utes pastured thousands of ponies on it in winter. To Meeker's surprise, Douglas objected heatedly to moving the agency there.

Meeker thought it over and concluded that this pony business did indeed present an obstacle to his whole bright plan for Ute salvation. The Utes, he perceived, were obsessed with these confounded ponies. They could never achieve the happiness which he held out to them as long as they had so many ponies to care for. It was a ticklish matter. And yet he was sure that Captain Armstrong had more than enough persuasive power to make the Indians see that the ponies were millstones around their necks.

And, sure enough, in the ensuing winter months, Douglas and Johnson let him have his way. The agency buildings were moved downstream to the richest part of Powell Park. Neat streets were laid out, ditches were dug, and forty acres of pony pasture were plowed, fenced, and planted to wheat. The young employees from Greeley built a nice house for Johnson and put cook stoves in the tepees of four families. Meeker's gentle daughter Josie induced three children to attend her agency school.

But serious trouble from outside the reservation came in the spring of 1879, and Meeker watched with mounting anguish as his dream faded. Colorado's new governor, Frederick W. Pitkin, had been elected on a Utes-Must-Go platform which he was trying hard to implement. The Denver papers were full of incendiary anti-Ute propaganda. Senator Teller forced Chief

CULVER SERVICE

Douglas, chief of the White River Utes.

Ouray's Uncompahgre band to sell 10,000 acres of prime farm land for $10,000—and failed to produce the promised money. It was a terribly dry spring. By mid-June the state's forests burned in hundreds of places, and the Teller crowd charged that the Utes had deliberately set all the fires.

At White River Agency the Indians took out their anger at all this unfairness toward them by ceasing to co-operate with Meeker further. And, as his dream collapsed, the agent's optimism faltered. His all-embracing love for his charges turned rapidly to hate. He spent much time alone nursing grudges against Douglas, against Johnson, against the ponies, even against his agency staff and his daughter Josie, who sided often with the Indians.

A particular irritation to him was the attitude of Arvilla Meeker's Ute housemaid, Jane. To say that this tall, pretty, bilingual girl of 22 disturbed Meeker is to understate probabilities. He had done everything he could to please her, including weeding her garden for six weeks in 1878 while she was off hunting. When she had returned, she had rewarded him with a sort of smile and nine beets out of a total crop of thirty bushels. In that tense spring of 1879, Meeker decided to coddle Jane no longer. He summoned her to his office one morning and began the conversation in a gentle kindly vein:

MEEKER: Now Jane, you will be planting your garden soon. I just want to warn you that last summer's style of gardening is played out.
JANE: Played out? How so?
MEEKER: Well, I'll tell you. After the things are planted, it will not do for you to run off and leave me to plow, hoe and pull weeds. You or some of your family must stay here all three moons and work your crops, for no one will touch them, and in that case you

will have nothing. Or they will be given to some other Indian to work and he will have all.

JANE: You say we must stay three moons? What for? Hoeing the things once is enough.

MEEKER: You must hoe them three or four times, and must keep watch of them and you need not undertake to tell me how the work is to be done.

JANE: But we never done so before and we had heaps.

MEEKER (warming up): But I tell you the thing is played out. If you get anything you must work for it.

JANE: Why can't white men do the work as before? They understand it. We don't.

MEEKER: It won't do. Now I worked your garden last year. I carried hundreds of pails of water to it. You had a nice garden and got lots of money. But this year we have a big ditch and plenty of water. You must attend to things yourself.

JANE (sweetly): But, Mr. Meeker, ain't you paid for working?

MEEKER: No. Not to work for you.

JANE: Well, what are you paid money for if not to work for us?

MEEKER (momentarily stumped): Yes, I see how it is. . . . I'll put it this way. I am paid to show you how to work.

JANE: But the Utes have a heap of money. What is the money for if it is not to have work done for us?

MEEKER (coming to a boil): I'll tell you, Jane. This money is to hire me and the rest of us to teach you to help yourselves so that you can be like white folks and get rich as they are rich—by work. You are not to be waited upon and supported in idleness all your lives. You have got to take hold and support yourselves or you will have trouble.

JANE (black eyes wide): Ain't all these cattle ours, and all this land?

MEEKER: The cattle, yes. The land, no.

JANE: Well, whose land is it, and whose is the money?

MEEKER (almost yelling): The land belongs to the government and is for your use, if you use it. If you won't use it and won't work, and if you expect me to weed your garden for you, white men away off will come in and by and by you will have nothing. This thing can't go on forever. As to money, it is to be used to make you helpful. It is time you turn to and take care of yourselves and have houses and stoves and chairs and beds and crockery and heaps of things. Do you understand?

JANE (very quiet): Yes. But I can't tell you, Mr. Meeker, how bad you make me feel.

She left the office and Meeker watched her straight proud form as she walked across the office porch, past his hitching rack and down the street which ended at Douglas' lodge on White River. She walked stiffly and rapidly, keeping her handsome head straight ahead.

We may guess that the agent was aware that he had said too much. He had asserted not only that the Utes didn't own White River valley, but that they couldn't even stay there if they didn't do what Meeker ordered them to do. And to make matters still worse, Meeker sat down now and wrote out the entire conversation verbatim for publication in the next issue of the Greeley *Tribune*.

Tension at the agency became so unbearable by early September that Meeker feared for the safety of Arvilla and Josie Meeker. But he would not call for troops from Fort Steele in Wyoming 200 miles away. The agent knew that to ask for soldiers would be to accept final defeat.

On the morning of September 8 he mailed a list of complaints to the Indian Office. Also, he called in the medicine man Johnson and accused him of stealing water for his ponies from Josie's school water barrel. Ponies! Always the ponies! Meeker was becoming psychopathic about them. Johnson denied stealing any water and left Meeker's office muttering. After lunch he returned and stood before the agent talking fast and loud. Meeker leaned easily back in his office chair, his pale blue eyes cold and a set smile on his weary face. He did not catch all that Johnson said, but it seemed to concern the plowing up of pony pasture and his suspicion that the agent was sending lies about the Utes to Washington.

Suddenly Meeker decided that he had heard enough. He raised an imperious hand and said, very deliberately, "The trouble is this, Johnson. You have too many ponies. You had better shoot some of them."

Johnson stared at the agent for a long moment, utterly dumfounded. Then his brown eyes blazed with the fire of a reasonable man who had just heard the consummation of blasphemy. He moved slowly toward Meeker, grasped his shoulders, lifted his long spare body from the chair and hustled him across the office and on to the porch. There, two employees ran up and grabbed Johnson as he flung Meeker hard against the hitching rack.

That was all. Johnson did not touch Meeker again. The agent tottered back to his chair, felt himself over and found that he was not badly hurt. Next day, he penned a telegraphic request to Washington for troops, stating that his life and those of his employees were in danger. As his courier rode north toward the Western Union office in Rawlins, Meeker must have known that his life's dream went with him.

In Washington the Indian Office passed Meeker's wire on to General Sherman who ordered a force of 153 soldiers and 25 civilians under Major Thomas T. Thornburgh to go to White River from Rawlins. Presumably the Major did not care for the task. As an army officer he detested the Indian Office and all its works. The Ute Agency was not even in his military department. He had no decent maps, no proper guides. He had had fighting experience only with Plains Indians. He knew nothing about these Utes, with whom he tended to sympathize.

The Major took his time. On Monday morning, September 29, his force reached the Ute Reservation line at Milk Creek, 25 miles north of White River. Thornburgh had exchanged messages earlier with Meeker and had agreed to ride alone over Yellowjacket Pass to the agency for talks with Douglas and Jack, leaving his soldiers outside the reservation. But he found that Milk Creek was almost dry because of the record drought. He had to have fresh water for his men and for his 400 animals. Therefore he ordered his force to move some miles into the reservation to a spot where water was available.

From the sage ridges above Milk Creek valley, Chief Jack and his band watched this unexpected movement with enraged astonishment. Suddenly the soldiers spied the Indians. Someone fired a gun. Then everyone was firing. Men began falling to earth. After some minutes Jack's courier leaped on his pony and galloped southward to bring the awful news to Douglas' band at the agency. Before noon Major Thornburgh, eleven of his troopers, and many Utes lay dead. Forty-odd white men were wounded. Nearly 300 army horses and mules were out of action. Without the use of these animals, the army survivors were completely trapped. They forted up behind their wagons and dead horses and barely managed to hold Jack's warriors off until relief troops arrived from Rawlins six days later.

On that same fateful Monday morning, everything seemed peaceful at White River Agency. The tension of recent weeks was as bad as ever, but the boys from Greeley and Douglas' men and the white women did their best to ignore it. Several young Utes loitered about begging biscuits at the big agency kitchen which Josie Meeker ran for the nine employees. She was helped by Flora Ellen Price, the plump, blond, teen-aged wife of Meeker's plowman. The agent, preoccupied and wan, spent all morning describing his difficulties in his September report. Soon after lunch he appeared at Josie's kitchen window to get from her the key to the government gun closet. He walked with a stoop again as in his unhappiest Greeley days. There was a grim smile on his strained face. And still he re-

tained enough of his old spirit to ask Josie if she knew what day September 29 was. When she shook her head, he said jauntily: "On this day in 1066, William the Conqueror landed in England!"

At 1:30 P.M. Josie, Arvilla, and Flora Ellen were still in the kitchen, washing and wiping the dinner dishes in the Indian summer heat. A small Ute boy stopped to borrow matches, announcing proudly, "Now I go smoke." Flora Ellen stepped outside to fetch her two small children. She saw some Greeley boys spreading dirt on the roof of a new building. Beyond them, on the street down to White River, she saw Douglas and a dozen of his men. Then she saw an Indian on a sweat-flecked pony galloping up to Douglas from the direction of Milk Creek.

The Indian said something to the old chief and immediately after that, Flora Ellen saw doom come. It came without signal, like the spontaneous firing at Milk Creek. Some of Douglas' men simply raised their Winchesters and began shooting at their white friends, the unarmed Greeley boys. Flora Ellen watched one boy fall from the new roof. She watched another as he begged the Utes not to shoot him. She saw her husband collapse holding his stomach. She snatched her crying children, joined the other women, and went with them and Frank Dresser, a Greeley boy, to the adobe milk house while the Indians fired some of the log buildings.

The three women, two children, and Dresser sat in the milk house for four hours, too stunned, too helpless, too hopeless to entirely comprehend the horror which was upon them. Arvilla Meeker picked at her faded calico dress, wept and stopped weeping, and prayed for her husband's safety. Josie was mixed sorrow and gentle compassion for the Utes, whom she had learned to understand. Flora Ellen was pure terror, dying the deaths of all the Indian-ravished heroines she had met in fiction.

At last they left the milk house in the cooling twi-

The Utes ambushed the troops sent to aid Meeker, an action that set off the agency attack. It was six days before a relief column lifted the siege.

light and ran back to Meeker's unburned house. In the agent's office, peaceful as a church, Josie stood a moment, a tall, slender, white-faced girl of 22, her lips parted in anguished query. She was staring at Pepys' Diary lying open on her father's desk where he had left it, apparently, just before stepping outside to investigate the firing. Through the window she saw Utes looting the agency storehouse. She said to the others, "Let's try to escape north while they are busy."

They went through the gate into Meeker's wheat field. Frank Dresser ran like a deer and disappeared in the sage, but later was wounded and died before he could reach help. The Utes saw the three women and the children and came for them. Arvilla fell when a bullet grazed her thigh and lay still on the ground. A young Ute named Thompson reached her and helped her to rise. "I am sorry," he said. "I am heap much sorry. Can you walk?"

Arvilla whispered, "Yes, sir."

The young Ute offered her his arm politely and led her toward White River. Near the agent's house, he asked if she had money inside.

"Very little."

"Please go and get money."

She limped into the quiet house calling "Papa! Papa!" and somehow found twenty-six dollars in bills and four dollars in silver. Then Thompson helped her to walk to Douglas near his tepee and she gave him the money. Near him was Josie on a pile of blankets holding little May Price on her lap. Further away were Flora Ellen and her son.

Arvilla limped from Ute captor to captor. Where, she asked, was the agent? The Utes shrugged. As night came on she watched the great full moon yellowing in the east. She began to shiver and she spoke to Douglas about the thin dresses she and the girls were wearing. Douglas told Thompson to take her back with a horse and lantern to get some things.

Meeker's house was burning at one end. Entering, Arvilla called, "Nathan!" but low and sorrowfully now, almost to herself. Then she loaded Thompson with warm clothes, towels, blankets, and a medicine box. She donned her hat and shawl, put a handkerchief and a needle packet in her pocket, and limped out hugging her big volume of *Pilgrim's Progress*.

A hundred yards south of the house she came suddenly on a man's dead body, startlingly white in the moonlight, and clad only in a shirt. It was Meeker. He had been shot in the side of his handsome head and a little blood trickled still from his mouth. But he lay entirely composed, straight as he had stood in life, his arms tranquil beside him as though he were about to tell Arvilla what had happened to William the Conqueror on September 29, 1066.

She cried softly and knelt to kiss him. But she did not actually kiss him. Young Thompson was beside her and she realized that he would not understand the gesture. Then she stood up and left the body, hop-

Frank Leslie's Illustrated Newspaper, FROM CULVER SERVICE

ing that Nathan Meeker's Utopia would be easier for him to come by in the land where he was now.

The massacre of Meeker and his eight young men by Douglas' band, the "ambush" of Thornburgh's soldiers by Jack's band, and the holding of the three white women as hostages for 23 days by both bands caused as much consternation as the Custer massacre in 1876. Millions of people were especially upset when the women testified after their rescue that Josie's person had been outraged repeatedly during their captivity, that Flora Ellen had been forced twice to submit, and that even old Douglas had insisted on "having connection" with Mrs. Meeker once.

The punishment of the alleged guilty was all the landgrabbers could have asked. The two White River bands were branded as criminals en masse by a political commission without any judicial powers whatever. Though only twenty White River Utes had staged the massacre, all 700 were penalized in that money owed to them by the government was paid instead to relatives of victims. Chief Ouray's Uncompahgre Utes, who had had nothing to do with the massacre or the "ambush," were held equally responsible. The 1868 treaty rights of all three bands were canceled. Their rights to be Americans as set forth in the Fourteenth Amendment were ignored. Title to their ancient Colorado homeland was extinguished and they were moved at gun point to barren lands in Utah. By these means the last and largest chunk of desirable Indian real estate was thrown open to white settlement.

And still, the year 1879 marked a happier turning point. It was the beginning of the end of indefensible white attitudes toward red men. Interior Secretary Carl Schurz was only one of many people who probed beneath the surface causes of the White River tragedy and then had the courage to say, and to keep on saying, that it would not have happened if the Utes had lived under the same laws as other Americans.

This novel notion took root and the roots spread far and wide. Before another decade passed, white men generally were agreeing that perhaps Indians were human beings too. Though the living Nathan Meeker failed to build his Utopia, in dying he made a contribution of far more value to his country than persuading an outdoor people to sleep in beds.

Marshall Sprague, a New York Times *correspondent, is the author of* Money Mountain, *the story of the Cripple Creek gold rush, and the recently published* Massacre: The Tragedy at White River *(Little, Brown & Co.).*

First by Land CONTINUED FROM PAGE 47

guide for the next day. At no time did Mackenzie's men actually have to repel an Indian attack; Mackenzie was almost invariably able to calm the hostility and fear of the Indians and in every case to continue his journey without disaster.

After nearly two weeks they reached a river called the Bella Coola by the local Indians, and from this friendly people Mackenzie was able to borrow a canoe and several braves. From village to village they hurried down the swift stream. On July 19, Mackenzie came upon a village of six houses built on palisades 25 feet high; when he climbed up to chat with the inhabitants, he could see the river emptying in the distance into a narrow blue-green arm of the sea.

In the morning the Bella Coola Indians were fearful of going with them further, for they probably were afraid of the warlike tribes who lived along the coast. Finally, however, two young Bella Coola braves went along to guide them in a large canoe. By 8 A.M. that day Mackenzie must have tasted the heady saltiness of the water, though the mouth of the channel was still out of sight.

They spent the night uneventfully on the shore of the channel, although the two Bella Coolas were extremely nervous and one of them actually deserted. The next morning they paddled onward many miles down the inlet (today called Dean Channel) without getting clear of the maze of inlets and islands. Mackenzie, satisfied that he had reached the sea, and worried by the low state of his provisions, decided that he should settle upon a good place from which to take his final astral readings, and then return immediately.

Just then three canoes bearing fifteen Indians approached them fearlessly and pulled alongside to study the explorer. Their leader, in a hostile manner, repeatedly informed Mackenzie that a white man named "Macubah" had come in a "large canoe" and fired upon him and his friends not long before. (Captain George Vancouver had been along that coast in a British vessel several weeks earlier.)

His behavior was most threatening, and Mackenzie, outnumbered, dared not risk a fight in the open. He ordered his men to paddle on toward a ruined village on shore where he hoped to take up a good defensive position, but the hostile Indians followed him and were joined by still other canoes. When they landed, the Europeans were surrounded by some fifty sullen warriors who loafed about, insolently poking and prying into their possessions. Finally they left toward sundown, not having mustered up enough anger to start a fight.

After an uneasy night, the *voyageurs* were anxious to depart, but Mackenzie wanted to spend an entire day double checking his navigation. His men begged and pleaded with him to let them get out at once, and the young Bella Coola Indian was so frantic that he actually foamed at the mouth. "Though I was not altogether free from apprehensions on the occasion," Mackenzie later noted in his driest possible British manner, "it was necessary for me to disguise them. My reply was . . . that I would not stir till I had accomplished my object."

In between his observations of the sun, Mackenzie melted some animal grease and mixed vermilion pigment in it; then on the face of a commanding rock he inscribed the words: "Alexander Mackenzie, from Canada, by land, the twenty-second of July, one thousand seven hundred and ninety-three." (The grease paint rapidly disappeared, but in our own century the place and the very rock have been relocated and identified.) At ten o'clock that night, when he had timed the emersion of the first satellite of Jupiter, he told the men he had finished his job; despite the darkness and their fatigue, the canoe was launched within minutes and the paddlers were speeding the frail craft up the channel with greedy strokes.

All night they continued, and shortly after dawn they landed near the village of the young Bella Coola Indian, who jumped out and ran for home.

Mackenzie followed swiftly, to see what the Indian was up to, but as he burst into a clearing before the stilt-legged houses, the Scotsman was set upon by two formerly friendly Bella Coolas carrying daggers. He raised his gun and they stood fast, while others joined them. The mystery was soon clear: their leader was none other than the coastal chieftain who had spoken about "Macubah," and who had evidently come here in the meantime to stir up trouble. Slowly the Indians encircled Mackenzie, and then one leaped upon him. The explorer jerked himself free, expecting to kill one or two before being slain, but at this moment one of his men emerged from the woods, and the Indians took flight, idiotically climbing up into their houses.

Assembling his men, Mackenzie, more angry than fearful, determined to frighten the Bella Coolas so that there would be no recurrence of the incident. With guns primed, he marched his men to the houses and ordered the young Bella Coola Indian down. When he descended, Mackenzie demanded the return of his hat and cloak and other articles which had been stolen in the scuffle plus a quantity of fish—yet true to his nature, he paid for the fish in goods. The Indians, thoroughly cowed, were vastly relieved to see him and his men pile into the canoe and paddle off eastward.

With this, the worst was over. On the return voyage, being lightly laden and familiar with the route, they sped along, passing from tribe to tribe in comparative peace. The several depots of buried food were in perfect order, the newly built canoe was waiting for them where they had left it, and the terrible portage at the Peace River Canyon, where they had cut their road over a mountain, was still in good condition.

On August 24, one month after starting back, and three and a half months after beginning this incredible trip, Mackenzie and his men rounded a turn on the Peace River and saw ahead their tiny palisaded home—Fork Fort, the winter outpost from which they had started in May. They broke out a flag and let off a fusillade of shots which brought the two caretakers rushing out to welcome them.

Mackenzie's great dream had now been realized and his fever was quenched. Detesting the boredom, suffering, and toil he had willingly endured, he soon returned to Montreal and busied himself in the management end of the fur trade, while he relished the pleasures of elegant clothing, a fine house, and a gay social life. In 1801 he published the journals of his two expeditions and with their appearance the civilized world came to regard him as a celebrity. Honors were heaped upon him, and King George III knighted him in 1802. From 1805 on, Sir Alexander lived chiefly in Scotland, where he married in 1812 and lived as the Laird of Avoch until his death in 1820.

Today his Fork Fort is marked by a simple monument with a bronze plaque, but the Indian villages he slept in have long since vanished without a trace. The trails he followed have been obliterated by time and the weather, or overlaid by modern roads, and few men ever see the rock on which he painted his name. For ironically enough, it is not at the scene of his great triumph that his name has been immortalized, but in the northern part of Canada where he first wrongly followed a river to the Arctic Ocean.

There, a vast chunk of remote, unpopulated land is called the District of Mackenzie, and the mighty Mackenzie Mountains and the Mackenzie River border it on the west.

And that is a paradox indeed, for he himself had named the river not the Mackenzie, but the Disappointment. His disappointment has made his name immortal; his achievement is almost forgotten.

Morton M. Hunt has been writing for magazines since his discharge from the Army Air Force after World War II. In 1956 he was president of the Society of Magazine Writers.

neer—he was indeed a lord. The steamboat pilot was a combination navigator and steersman and a regular full-time officer aboard the vessel.

The captain was the boss of the boat. He was often its owner or part owner. It was he who arranged for the safety and comfort of the passengers, inspired confidence, and spread charm among the ladies—and he had to know every trick of the trade to stay in a highly competitive business. Of the hundreds of captains who commanded steamboats on the Mississippi perhaps the best known and most colorful was Captain Thomas P. Leathers.

Tom Leathers was born in 1816 in Kentucky; coming down the Mississippi in 1836, he and a brother began steamboating on the Yazoo River in a boat called the *Sunflower*. By 1840 he, another brother, and their associates built the *Princess*, the first of five

boats by that name that they ran in the New Orleans-Vicksburg trade. In 1845 Leathers built the first *Natchez;* three years later he sold her and built another, larger, and finer *Natchez*. This boat, too, was soon superseded by a third *Natchez* which unfortunately burned in 1854 while at the New Orleans levee. Tom Leathers' brother James died in that fire, and Captain Tom and his young wife barely escaped with their lives.

A fourth *Natchez* was soon built and placed in the trade. This boat proudly flew the U.S. Mail pennant, more and more business came its way, and soon the fourth *Natchez* was too small to suit her owner.

Shortly before the Civil War broke out, Leathers built the fifth *Natchez*. She was a beauty, the finest thing afloat on the Mississippi. Captain Leathers proudly showed her off, but, alas, not for long. After only a few months of service, New Orleans fell to Farragut, and Leathers sent the *Natchez* up to the Yazoo River to escape capture. Used as a ram during the war, the fifth *Natchez* was eventually burned.

After the war Leathers slowly recouped his fortunes. In 1869 he built his sixth *Natchez*, the racer. She, too, was a beautiful boat—as long as a New Orleans city block, with immense paddle wheels 43 feet in diameter

driven by high-pressure steam engines capable of producing about 2,000 horsepower. It was said that she was as graceful in appearance on the water as a swan. Leathers mounted her whistle, which sounded like a huge bumblebee, on the inside of one of the smokestacks near the top. "The whistle is for awakening persons on shore, not on the steamboat," said he.

Leathers had high standards in the conduct of his steamboat business; his boats were swift, they ran on schedule, and no detail was overlooked to make travel and transportation safe and sure. Moreover, Leathers had a flair for publicity that would have delighted a public relations man. He knew how to dramatize himself and his boats. For instance, the tall stacks of the *Natchez* were painted red, enabling anyone to spot his boat in the forest of sooty cylinders on the New Orleans waterfront.

Physically, Leathers was tall and well proportioned—a really big man. He had a heavy head of hair and always wore a beard. His face was not handsome, but a forceful one dominated by a firm, almost obstinate jaw. He habitually wore a ruffled shirt ornamented by a diamond cluster pin; his suits were of Confederate gray and he was an unreconstructed southerner who would not fly the American flag on his boats. In fact, he refused to recognize that the war was over until March 4, 1885, when at Vicksburg, he decided to bury the hatchet. The Democrats had won the election, so Leathers fired the cannon from the forecastle of his boat, and amid a celebration, declared the war ended, hoisting the flag which for some 24 years had not graced the jack staff of his boats.

In 1870 Leathers was in his prime as a steamboat captain—extremely self-confident about his *Natchez* and about himself. His one-time friend and associate but now bitter rival, Captain John W. Cannon, was running the *Rob't E. Lee* when the sixth *Natchez* came out. Looking about for a spectacular coup to dramatize the superiority of the *Natchez* over the *Lee*, Leathers pushed the *Natchez* from New Orleans to St. Louis and broke the record of three days, twenty-three hours, and nine minutes which had been made in 1844 by the fast *J. M. White*. This brought matters to a head and although both steamboatmen denied they were racing, both started for St. Louis on June 30, 1870, within minutes of each other. Cannon had set about in earnest to win the race. He stripped his boat, took no freight, and arranged to refuel in midstream. Leathers, too sure of himself, took on a load of cargo and made no extraordinary preparations for the race.

The boats were probably fairly well matched as to speed, everything else being equal, but the Admiral of the Mississippi was outguessed and outfoxed by the wily Cannon. The *Natchez* lost the race, undoubtedly the most exciting ever to be staged on the Mississippi, but to his dying day Captain Leathers would not admit that his was the slower boat.

The sixth *Natchez* operated some nine and a half years. In that time she made 401 round trips in the New Orleans-Vicksburg trade. She could carry 5,500 bales of cotton each trip, besides other freight and passengers, and could negotiate the distance between New Orleans and Natchez in sixteen and a half hours.

Leathers built a seventh *Natchez* when the sixth wore out, and she, too, was a big, handsome boat. For many years on Saturday afternoon at exactly five o'clock, he would appear on her boiler deck roof, vigorously tap his big bell for departure, and the *Natchez* would move out proudly from the landing, glide slowly downstream as far as the Mint, turn about, pause a moment, and then with black smoke pouring from her tall red stacks, speed swiftly up the river, firing her cannon and lowering her flag as she steamed past Canal Street. No wonder there was always a crowd at the levee in those days!

The seventh *Natchez* was a little too late for the big time. She did well at first but the plush days were past, and in 1887 Leathers had to lay her up because there was not enough business to keep her going.

For a man who had braved the river for sixty years, Leathers met a landsman's death. When he was eighty years old, he was knocked down by a "scorcher," which is what they called a hit-and-run bicyclist in 1896, and died of his injuries on June 13 of that year.

Steamboat races were generally impromptu affairs rather than staged races over long distances. To passengers, often bored by the monotony of a long trip and confinement in close quarters, racing was a thrill indeed, whatever the outcome. Everybody knew it was dangerous, from the captain on down, yet it was difficult not to yield to temptation when two well-matched boats came abreast of each other.

To those on shore, a steamboat race was a dazzling sight. To see two steamboats with flags flying, smoke rolling from tall chimneys, steam spurting from the 'scape pipes, foam flying from their bows, passengers and crews yelling, was a sight to be remembered.

In March, 1858, occurred a spectacular race which was probably the longest and most animated ever to be run on the Mississippi. This was the race between the *Baltic* and the *Diana*. Both boats left within two minutes of each other from New Orleans one Sunday morning, headed for Louisville, 1,382 miles away. So

closely matched were they in speed that they were in sight of each other a great part of the way. At one time, near Point Worthington, the two boats "locked horns" and for some fifteen miles ran neck and neck together. The *Baltic* was the faster boat and she won the race; time: five days, six hours, twenty-two minutes.

There were much faster boats than the *Baltic;* one of these was the *Peytona*, a stepper in the New Orleans-Louisville trade. Joe Stealey, an old-time steamboatman reminisced in 1887 about a trip he had made aboard this boat in the fifties: "I was on the *Peytona*, when she made what I believe to be the swiftest time any steamboat had to her credit. She was coming up the Lower Mississippi, against the current, mind you. Old Captain Shallcross was her master. We all knew she was a fast boat, but the Captain would not let the boys put her to her best. One day, it being very warm, he lay down in the cabin and went to sleep. The boys determined to see how fast the *Peytona* would go. It was just forty miles to Converse, and therefore we knew how to calculate. They put on all steam and reached Converse in two hours, making twenty miles an hour. Captain Shallcross woke up at Converse and wouldn't let the boys run her any further—but that was enough."

The steamboat age was noted for the food served aboard the boats. Silverware, china, and linens were often made especially for the crack packets and menus set a standard probably never equalled since. For Christmas dinner in 1859, Captain Leathers' fifth *Natchez* had a gaily printed bill of fare offering, among the fourteen courses, four types of fish, six broiled meats and six kinds of roasts, eight entrees and nine cold dishes, five types of game, and thirty-six different desserts.

Then came the Civil War, bringing an almost complete disruption to commercial steamboat traffic on the Mississippi. When it was over, the finest of the prewar packets, which had holed up in tributary streams like the Yazoo, were gone forever—destroyed by the Confederates themselves to avoid capture or sunk in conflict. But this was not the death knell of steamboating—in a few years bigger and better boats, like the *Ruth*, the *Richmond*, the *Rob't E. Lee*, the *Great Republic*, and the incomparable *J. M. White*, made their appearance, and for a long time steamboating seemed to have caught its second wind. "But the railroad, which runs in high water or low and does not snag itself in a vital spot with a snag, came along and cleared the steamboat out of business," wrote Clyde Fitch, a newspaperman who saw the transition take place. By the 1880's, the signs of dissolution were everywhere apparent; in the 1890's more and more boats went to the bank, never to return; in 1909 there were no longer any through Mississippi packet lines and steamboating was dying fast.

Some people live beyond their time; such a man was Captain LeVerier Cooley, one of the very last of the old-time lower Mississippi steamboatmen. Captain Cooley "learned" the river in the 1870's and trod the decks of steamboats until he died, December 19, 1931. He ran the *Tensas*, pronounced Ten-saw (which carried a big circular saw swung between its chimneys with a numeral ten painted on it), in the 1880's; the

big *Ouachita* in the nineties, the sturdy *America* in the first two decades of the 1900's, and his last, the "little" *Ouachita* in the twenties.

Captain Cooley, who ran his boats from New Orleans to Vicksburg and later up the Ouachita and Black rivers, carried tremendous quantities of cotton to market almost until the end. He once estimated that he had handled 800,000 bales of cotton on the *America* alone, besides large quantities of other cargo. The *America* he loved best of all his boats and when he died, the huge deck bell which had tapped departure time for so many years was used as a monument over his grave in New Orleans—a fitting marker for a steamboatman and the end of an era.

Leonard V. Huber, a New Orleans collector and historian, is co-author of several books—The Great Mail *(1949),* Louisiana Purchase *(1953), and* Tales of the Mississippi *(1955).*

The Sergeant Major's Strange Mission CONTINUED FROM PAGE 29

ness, Arnold suddenly confronted him with an order: he was to embark at once with the rest of the Loyalist Legion on the transports in the harbor for a voyage to Virginia. The long-deferred British expedition to the Chesapeake was under way.

Champe was trapped. There was nothing to do but join the troops toiling up the gangplanks, and there was no time to notify Mr. Baldwin. The opportunity for seizing Arnold was snatched away by a coincidence of timing; that night Continental soldiers waited in Bergen Woods in vain.

After a violent sea passage, Arnold's transports disgorged their battered troops and surviving horses in the James River on January 4, 1781. And while Arnold, the American traitor, burned and pillaged Virginia, John Champe reluctantly marched with him. If it were not enough that Champe's painfully nurtured plans had been smashed, he now was compelled to war against his own country and comrades. It was entirely possible that he might face his own corps in battle. If captured and identified as a former American soldier, he faced summary trial and execution unless he could somehow get word to Henry Lee, the only man in the Southern Department who knew that his desertion had been staged under the authority of the Commander in Chief. Desertion from the British Army held almost as much peril, for if caught he would be hanged by them as a deserter. However, he decided he had to chance it; he had to escape and attempt to make his way to Lee's Legion, somewhere in the Carolinas.

So sometime before Arnold was recalled to New York in late spring, John Champe deserted from the British camp as skillfully as he once had from his own. How long he traveled the back roads of Virginia and the Carolinas no one was ever to know. Henry Lee later recalled it was May when Champe showed up at the Legion camp on the Congaree River.

Although his mission had failed, Champe had performed an extraordinary duty with faithfulness, courage, and daring. In order to prevent his being taken in battle by the enemy and hanged, Lee granted him an honorary discharge, and sent him as a civilian back to the remote security of Loudoun County, Virginia, to sit out the rest of the war.

Had Sergeant Champe succeeded in taking Arnold, he would at least have won his promotion. As it turned out, he received no reward whatever. He died years before the Congress, in 1818, established pensions for Revolutionary veterans, although his widow in 1837, when nearly eighty, was granted $120 per annum as the needy relict of a Revolutionary soldier. Ironically, however, in 1847, Sergeant Champe was awarded a sort of posthumous promotion: that year, in consideration of his special service, the Congress of the United States granted his descendants an amount equal to the commutation pay of an ensign in the Continental service.

George F. Scheer, a specialist in Revolutionary War history, is co-author with Hugh F. Rankin of Rebels and Redcoats, *which was the* AMERICAN HERITAGE *book selection in our February issue.*

Churchman
of the Desert

CONTINUED FROM PAGE 35

time farmers came in swelling numbers to raise cereals.

Sometimes abroad in winter he found it necessary to walk up and down all night by a campfire to escape freezing to death. Only too often, taken ill on his lonely journeys, he fought to overcome his body's weakness with his strong will. And knowing his immense land in the same terms as any other frontiersman, he loved it the more for seeking out, and surviving, its hazard and its challenge.

In August of 1866 Lamy gave to Rome an accounting of his first sixteen years in the old river kingdom. Civilization was emerging under his touch. As people in old Mexican towns and Indian pueblos came to know him well, and to feel his interest, the parishes revived. The spirit of growth in religion created growth in all other beneficial expressions of society. By a simple extension of his own character, the Bishop also created for the old Spanish kingdom a sense of social enlightenment through which, for the first time in all her three centuries, her people could advance their condition and so come to be masters instead of victims of their environment.

In 1853 the vicariate apostolic had been raised to the rank of diocese and a year later the Bishop had gone to France on the first of the many journeys taken by himself and later by Machebeuf to enlist young priests for the tasks in New Mexico. New Mexico, he reported in 1866, had 110,000 Mexicans and 15,000 Catholic Indians. To serve the great diocese he now had 41 priests where he had arrived to find 9. Most of the ruined churches had been repaired, and he had built 85 new ones, and the total number was 135. They were all made of earth and had "no architectural character" and were as poor inside as out. But—what mattered to him—they were "well frequented."

And so were the schools. He now had three in Santa Fe "in full prosperity, with never fewer than two hundred pupils, and often three hundred." In almost every mission there was one school, and in some, several. There were now five Lorettine convents and academies in the diocese, and on New Year's Day, 1866, four nuns of St. Vincent de Paul opened the first orphanage and hospital in New Mexico, using the Bishop's own house which he gave up to the purpose.

All these signs of compassionate belief in the dignity of human beings and their right to growth were made against the familiar background of primitive techniques and general poverty in the New Mexico Rio Grande country. His plans prospered, and there was good will all about him, for everyone, including non-Catholics—like the military commander of New Mexico who gave him $1,000 toward the new orphanage— was eager to help him in his work.

There was one detail he did not trouble to include in his report. In 1863 he had worked for the passage of the first Public School Act of New Mexico, and when it became law, he was, along with the territorial governor and the secretary of state, a member of the commission erected by the legislature to administer it. Only a few years before, given an earlier chance to vote on the creation of free schools, the citizens had defeated the measure. The social climate had changed with the general effort at enlightenment under his example.

Increasing settlement of the West added heavy burdens to the work of the See of Santa Fe. In 1867, upon Lamy's recommendation, Colorado was detached from the diocese and given its own vicar apostolic—Machebeuf, who in his turn received the miter. A year later Arizona was similarly organized, with Father Juan B. Salpointe as vicar apostolic. In 1869 Bishop Salpointe presented himself at Rome, in company with Bishop Machebeuf, and the two were closely questioned by Pius IX about their vast outlands.

Returning through France, their fatherland, they paused to do an errand for the Bishop of Santa Fe. When Bishop Salpointe arrived home in the Southwest, he was able to say that the errand was done, for he had arranged for French architects Antoine and Projectus Mouly, father and son, and several skilled stonecutters, to come to Santa Fe where they would build out of native rock the Cathedral of Saint Francis.

On Wednesday, June 16, 1875, at daybreak, cannonading sounded over Santa Fe in salute from Fort Marcy. Shortly afterward the students' band of music from Saint Michael's College came before the Bishop's house to serenade him. In the streets, which were decorated with evergreens, small boys set off firecrackers, while the bells of the still unfinished cathedral and the other churches sent out widening rings of sound that met in the brilliant air.

The old capital was beginning its greatest day of jubilee, for it was celebrating the elevation of the diocese of Santa Fe to the rank of a metropolitan see, and Juan Bautista Lamy was appointed by Pope Pius IX to be its first archbishop. Everyone took part in the jubilee—the civil government, the military forces, the public, and a great gathering of clergy, headed by Bishop Salpointe, who bestowed the pallium that had come from Rome, and Bishop Machebeuf, who sang the Pontifical High Mass in the courtyard of St. Michael's College. A grand luncheon was held in the Archbishop's garden, where the 8th Cavalry band played lively airs among the trees.

At a suitable moment William G. Ritch, the acting territorial governor of New Mexico, rose to read a speech which he later sent to the New York *Herald*. Sketching the history of New Mexico, he was happy to see present some lineal descendants of Alvar Nuñez Cabeza de Vaca, who in 1535 was the first European to set foot on New Mexican land. The Governor then described conditions as the Archbishop had found them and catalogued the improvements which had come about under his touch.

"The reforms, the general elevation of the moral tone and the general progress that has been effected since the American occupation," he said, "are very largely, and in some cases entirely, due to the judicious ecclesiastical administration and to the wholesome precepts and examples which have shone forth upon this people from the living presence of the Archbishop of Santa Fe . . . whom we all know, and know only to admire and respect."

When evening fell there were speeches in the plaza in Spanish and English, and more band music by the cavalry musicians, and bonfires, fireworks, and a balloon ascension, and illuminated transparencies of Pius IX, the Archbishop and the two visiting bishops. Late at night all ended with a torchlight procession.

A day later, when the Archbishop's garden was cleared of the clutter of celebration, it was once again a retreat where every tree and raked bed and flowing water course showed something of the abiding joy of its master in the materials of natural life as they were brought to growth and usefulness.

There as he grew older the Archbishop spent happy and busy hours. His garden was walled with adobe. Extending for about five acres around his plain small town house with its private chapel south of the cathedral, the garden was laid out with a playing fountain, a sundial on a pedestal of Santa Fe marble, and aisles of trees, plants, and arbors. Formal walks led from one end of the garden to the other, with little bypaths turning aside among the flower beds and leading to cunningly placed benches in the shade. To the west through the branches of his trees he could make out the long blue sweep of the Jemez Mountains. At the south end of the garden on its highest ground was a pond covering half an acre, fed by a spring. Trout lived in the pond and came to take crumbs which the Archbishop threw to them. Now and then he would send a mess of trout over to St. Michael's College to be cooked for the boys.

From the first the Archbishop had been interested in the approach of the Atchison, Topeka and Santa Fe railroad into New Mexico. After traveling thousands and thousands of miles on the back of a horse throughout a quarter of a century of pastoral visits—he called it "purgatorial work"—he knew better than most men what the railroad would do for the development of archdiocese and territory. But as the tracks crept forward from the east a mile or two a day in 1879, reaching toward the Rio Grande, it became known that they would bypass Santa Fe.

The leaders of Santa Fe were concerned, foremost among them the Archbishop. If the railroad would not route its main line through the capital, then a seventeen-mile branch line must be built to connect the two; and if the railroad would not budget funds to build such a branch line, then let the citizens of Santa Fe raise the money to pay for the job. He headed a petition calling for a bond issue election to authorize the expenditure of $150,000 for the branch line. The election was held, the issue was carried by a three to one vote, and on February 9, 1880, Territorial Governor Lew Wallace drove the last spike in the new spur. The junction point on the main line was named Lamy.

The city at large knew him as a friend. When he passed through the plaza he stopped to speak to all who greeted him. If citizens were locked in stubborn dispute, he was sometimes called upon to compose their quarrels. A fellow citizen once said of him in a speech that he was the greatest peacemaker he knew.

He had a fine sense of the past. Once when there was a movement by progressive citizens to tear down the old Palace of the Governors on the plaza in order to build on its site a new territorial capital, he opposed the destruction of that repository of so much history, and others joined with him to save it.

As there was a time to take up work, so was there a time to lay it down. On February 19, 1885, Bishop Salpointe came to Santa Fe from Arizona as coadjutor to the Archbishop with right of succession. On July 18, the bishop coadjutor took over the affairs of the archdiocese. The act could mean only one thing. It was explained in a letter which Archbishop Lamy sat down to write at Santa Fe on August 26. On Sunday, September 1, 1885, in every parish the priest unfolded the pastoral letter and read aloud the expected but still affecting news. The first, the great, Archbishop of Santa Fe had retired.

But if now he was free to take his ease at the Villa Pintoresca, his little rural lodge at Tesuque, four miles from Santa Fe, it was not long until he was off again on his Father's business. In May, 1886, he blessed the nearly completed cathedral and then set

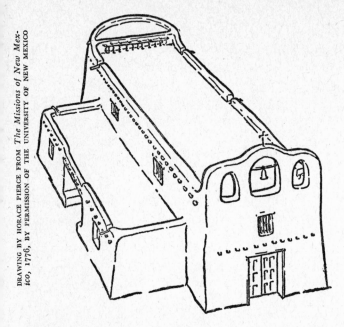

DRAWING BY HORACE PIERCE FROM *The Missions of New Mexico*, 1776, BY PERMISSION OF THE UNIVERSITY OF NEW MEXICO

out for Mexico to raise more funds for its last additions. He was 72. The journey took him across 10,000 miles, and once beyond El Paso, he traveled almost entirely by mule or horse. On a certain day he rode over thirty miles in high mountains on difficult trails, wearing a shawl against the chill of the thin air. On that day he confirmed over 1,000 people, and during the whole journey 35,000.

During the decades after the Mexican War, civilization came to the old Latin kingdom of the Southwest. It was the product principally of two agents—one, the government of the United States in all its formal expressions of law and administration; the other, Archbishop Lamy and the energetic example of his dutiful faith. Neither could have succeeded so well without the other. Both kept pace with the increase in population and consequent social need.

Both met and survived various threats of violence—the furies of the last Indian wars, the Civil War with its Confederate invasion of New Mexico happily defeated in a single campaign, the murderous extravagances of outlaws who succeeded too long in holding cheaply human life and safety. Together the separate but harmonious governments of Church and State worked to bring the vast southwestern frontier into the frame of peace and order.

On October 4, 1887, Juan Bautista Lamy appeared in Santa Fe to keep the feast of Saint Francis of Assisi. There was a procession that evening. Little stacks of piñon wood burned along the streets, throwing firelight like banners across adobe buildings. The marchers carried lighted candles through the sharp autumn air. In the procession walked the retired archbishop, and it was a wonder to see him again—so thin and white, so frail and faithful—passing through his streets

to the cathedral for vespers at the end of the feast. He was back again on December 12 to dedicate the chapel of Loretto Convent, now at last completed. The cathedral was not finished—but it was in continuous use, and the choir of Saint Michael's College sang the midnight Mass there at Christmas.

A week or so later in January, 1888, a message came from the Villa Pintoresca. The old archbishop had been taken ill in the country and asked to be brought into town, where his cold—he said he had a heavy cold—might be treated properly. A carriage was sent at once. He was brought to his old, high, square room in the Archbishop's house where the white plaster walls were finished at the ceiling with plaster cherubim. It was plain that he suffered from pneumonia. At first he seemed to recover, but relapses followed and early in the morning of February 13 all the bells of Santa Fe began to toll, and soon everyone in the old mountain capital knew for whom. He died mildly after having received the last sacraments from his successor, Archbishop Salpointe. He was 74 years old. He had been a priest for 50 years, a bishop for 38.

Robed in pontifical vestments, his body was laid first in the Loretto Chapel. From there it was taken in procession around the plaza to the cathedral, which it was never to leave again. For 24 hours it lay in mitered state before the high altar where 6,000 people came to pass by it in candlelight. One who kept vigil was Joseph Machebeuf. On February 16 was sung the pontifical Requiem Mass. It was the last occasion to draw the two prelates together, one in life, the other in death.

When it was time for a sermon, Joseph Machebeuf came forward to give it. As fast as memories ran through his mind, tears ran down his deeply marked face, and he found it difficult to speak. He remembered what they had passed through together, the two seminarians, the two missioners, the two vicars, and what together they had transformed in the immense land where they had spent themselves for the lives, mortal and immortal, of others.

Presently, the tremendous liturgy of the dead was resumed which by its impersonality brought a sense of triumph over death; and the body of the Archbishop was laid into a crypt before the high altar of the church which the generations have made into the monument over his grave.

A year later Bishop Machebeuf died in Denver.

Paul Horgan has spent much of his life in New Mexico and has written extensively about the Southwest. Portions of his Pulitzer Prize-winning history of the Rio Grande, Great River, *appeared in the first issue of* AMERICAN HERITAGE. *He is now at work on a biography of Archbishop Lamy.*

When the President Disappeared

CONTINUED FROM PAGE 13

up from New York to make impressions, and he quickly fashioned a hard-rubber plug for the gaping jaw hole.

Despite his continuing discomfort, by July 12 Cleveland was doggedly at work on his message to Congress for August 7. It went slowly. He had got little done by the seventeenth, when Joe Bryant ordained another trip to sea in the *Oneida*. This time their object was, again in utmost secrecy, to remove the rubber plug and see how the wound was healing. As they had feared, patches of evil tissue were regrowing; so they managed another gas job by themselves as Dr. Bryant scraped the hole with thorough diligence.

Back ashore, where the press had not missed him, Cleveland yielded to Dan Lamont's insistence that the

---

DR. KEEN MAKES ANOTHER APPEARANCE

Twenty-eight years later, at the age of 84, the surgeon who helped save President Cleveland appeared again at an important medical moment in the annals of the presidency, although he could not have known it at the time. In August, 1921, while vacationing nearby, Dr. Keen was summoned to Campobello Island in New Brunswick, Canada, as a consultant in diagnosing Franklin D. Roosevelt, who had, apparently, caught cold after extensive sailing, running, and swimming in the frigid Bay of Fundy. The second day Roosevelt lost the ability to move his legs, and Keen, examining him the third day, according to a letter from Mrs. Roosevelt (*F.D.R.: His Personal Letters, Vol. II*), concluded "that a clot of blood from a sudden congestion has settled in the lower spinal cord temporarily removing the power to move though not to feel." He prescribed massage and predicted that recovery might "take some months." Mrs. Roosevelt added, "He also sent his bill for $600!" As Roosevelt's condition worsened over the next few days, Keen altered his diagnosis from a clot to a "lesion" in the spinal cord. It was some days before other doctors discovered that Roosevelt in fact had infantile paralysis, for which, of course, massage was the wrong treatment.

—Based on an article by Noah D. Fabricant, M.D., on the possible causal relationship between tonsillectomy and poliomyelitis (F.D.R.'s tonsils had been removed not long before), in Eye, Ear, Nose & Throat Monthly, *June, 1957.*

---

attorney general be allowed to come up and help with the message to Congress. When Richard Olney arrived he was shocked to see how haggard the round face had become, how gaunt the robust body. "My God, Olney, they nearly killed me!" grunted Cleveland, and went to work on the draft speech Olney had brought with him. He retained only about one-sixth of it, writing the rest of 2,800 words himself in his own laborious longhand.

With the advent of August, Cleveland was still feeling miserable, but he insisted on journeying back to Washington not later than the fifth. He wanted a couple of days to collar returning members of Congress and impress upon them their duty to pass the Sherman Act repealer with all speed. The Senate, Lord knew, would be trouble enough, but the House must not hesitate.

The Congress met on the seventh and duly received the President's uncompromising message. ". . . The operation of the silver purchase law now in force," he wrote, "leads in the direction of the entire substitution of silver for gold in the Government Treasury, and . . . this must be followed by the payment of all Government obligations in depreciated silver. . . .

"The people of the United States are entitled to a sound and stable currency, and to money recognized as such on every exchange and in every market of the world. Their government has no right to injure them by financial experiments opposed to the policy and practice of other civilized states."

Cleveland stayed in hot Washington four more days. Then, with the repealer measure introduced, and all his personal pressures to bear, he crept back to Gray Gables to resume getting well.

Meantime, on the very day he went to Washington, something occurred in New York City which came very near to unmasking Cleveland's entire high conspiracy.

When the disgruntled Dr. Hasbrouck left the *Oneida* at New London, it was to assist a very high-toned medico indeed named Leander P. Jones, vet to the blue bloods of Newport and Manhattan. To save skin off his own nose, Hasbrouck let Jones know just who and what had detained him.

Miffed at being treated so highhandedly, even by Dr. Joe Bryant and the President of the United States, Dr. Jones tipped off a newspaper friend of his, one E. J. Edwards, a reporter for the Philadelphia *Press*, who signed all his work rather grandly "Holland."

102

Gray Gables, the Clevelands' summer home on Buzzard's Bay, served as a salubrious haven for the President's recovery.

Holland wasted no time getting up to 147 West 126th Street. There Dr. Hasbrouck, persuaded that the story was publicly known at least in outline, and far from ashamed of his own conspicuous part in it, confirmed it to Holland in full detail.

Thus, just four days before his fight in Congress began and in time for the grave question about his health to affect the fight perhaps fatally, Cleveland's secret was out.

And yet it wasn't out—not quite. As conscientious as he was alert, Holland sought to check his colossal scoop. Imperatively his sources must be Dr. Bryant, Dr. Keen, Dan Lamont, and the White House.

For his pains poor Holland was rebuffed by all these sources as a scandal-mongering scoundrel, and Dr. Hasbrouck branded a vicious prevaricator, an unknown dentist who had been called in on a routine extraction job and been fired for bungling.

The publishers of the Philadelphia *Press* withheld the story. Not for nearly four weeks did they get up enough confirmation and nerve to print it. By that time the huge white lie that it exposed had succeeded and changed places with the truth.

Congressman William Jennings Bryan orated for three hours on August 16 against the repealer (warming up for his "Cross of Gold" speech three years later) but on August 28 the House voted 239 to 108 in Cleveland's favor. When the Holland story came out next day, it had been so bruited about and discredited in advance that, though it was widely quoted, the conspirators' denials were quoted also and preponderantly believed.

Helpful also in supporting his great deception through its final stage was Cleveland's health. With more rest, fishing, and sea air, he now rebounded. By September 5 he was in shape to address a Pan-Amer-

ican Medical Congress in Washington, at which the most jaundiced professional eye could but agree that he never looked livelier or more robust. Keen's cheek retractor had obviated any outward scar. Gibson's refitted jaw plug filled any telltale hollow and, if anything, improved his always heavy diction. And on September 9 his wife bore the President, who was only 52 and now looked it again, another girl child.

In the Senate the final victory of Gold over Silver, and the beginning of the end of the earthquake, came less through Cleveland's efforts than through the Silverites' own folly. With the little Vice President's connivance, they filibustered so long—and so absurdly —that by October 30 enough in-betweeners were fed up to make the vote 48 to 37.

So ended an arch cabal in allegiance to the nation's well-being. As to its violence to veracity, that was not mended until 1917. Then, with most of the other principals dead (Cleveland of heart trouble, and not one more trace of cancer, in 1908), aged Dr. Keen found it fit and profitable to publish a book telling the whole story.

E. J. (Holland) Edwards was long dead, too, and still dishonored. But the press which had reviled him now made such amends as it could. Failing a marble monument, it at least erected in his memory a paramount policy from which it is doubtful that any President will ever find it possible again to escape: the full and instant truth about the White House occupant's whereabouts and his health.

John Stuart Martin is a former managing editor of Time, *author of a novel,* General Manpower, *a picture history of Russia and many magazine articles. He lives at Great Meadows, New Jersey, where he operates a commercial shooting preserve.*

Whither the Course of Empire?

CONTINUED FROM PAGE 61

yond the imagination of people who had not experienced it. To let in the sun was the necessary beginning of the pioneer's corn patch. And the course of empire was westward, in spite of the trees.

So, while Cole, Bryant, and Cooper courted the Muse of Nature their industrious countrymen persisted in raping the wilderness with lusty abandon. "They are cutting down all the trees in the beautiful valley on which I have looked so often with a loving eye," Cole wrote his patron; ". . . maledictions on all our dollar-goaded utilitarians." The woods along the Hudson were beginning to seem just as perishable as the cliffs and walls at Volterra. And far beyond the reach of his eye—all the way now to Oregon and California—the empire builders were rearing an unsightly superstructure on the face of the virgin earth. Never before in history was the nature of such a large part of the world so radically and rapidly transformed by human industry as it was to be in America. The proud boasts of the continent's conquerors were issued in the same breath with the hymns to Nature; sometimes, with touching irony, out of the same mouth.

"Yankee enterprise has little sympathy with the picturesque," warned one reviewer in 1847, "and it behooves our artists to rescue from its grasp the little that is left, before it is forever too late." Years earlier Audubon had felt that bitter urgency as he noted the inexorable thrust of civilization into the forested homes of his beloved birds. No one, he realized, would ever again be able to see the birds of America as he had seen them and drawn them—and, more than once, slaughtered them beyond all need.

In all this there was a conflict of principle that tore at the conscience of Cole's and Emerson's generation. America's Manifest Destiny was, as the *Democratic Review* defined it in coining the phrase, "to overspread the continent allotted by Providence for the free development of our yearly multiplying millions." This was part of our national mission, acclaimed by patriotic fervor and supported by scriptural authority. One could invoke the ancient distinctions between nature and grace avowed in the Calvinist theology of the Yankee Puritans. To equate the mastery of Nature with the mastery of destiny was a simple operation for the vaunters of progressive democracy.

But the older orthodoxies of religion and the newer orthodoxies of democracy were alike confounded by the romantic veneration of Nature. One could, after all, learn more of mortal evil and of good in one impulse from a vernal wood than from the prescribed authorities, as Wordsworth so sweetly argued; the world of man is too much with us for the good of our immortal souls. It is in Nature, as Emerson reflected, that our spirits will find their true emancipation.

If, as so many agreed, to maintain its unique character and to hold to its great promise America must avoid the "debauching artificialities" of civilization that so surely had corroded all older societies, how could one—without becoming schizophrenic—accept its booming progress that leveled the forests and gouged the hills and that was also its Messianic mission? One could disguise the issue with euphemisms and describe the materialistic speculation as "an immense exertion of the spirit," as Mr. Miller points out was done. One could shirk the whole problem in a blind faith that somehow, by some peculiar law of nature not clearly formulated or previously applied, things would work out all right in America. (*Laissez faire* were the magic words.) Or one could wrestle with the question, as Cole did in *The Course of Empire,* and express the gloomy suspicion that in the end "Time's noblest offspring" would pay the same price as the Medes and Persians, Etruscans and Mayans, for arrogantly heaping their civilizations on Nature.

Which is to say that his mood was somewhat deeper than the endemic melancholy of romanticism. It is possible to believe, in any case, that his allegory was pointed and, judging from its reception by the more sensitive minds of the day, that it reflected a general foreboding. Could one, with impunity, attempt to build a heaven on earth, as Americans seemed bent to do? Was this roaring material "progress" truly compatible with our national virtue? It is hard to determine whether Cole was more disturbed by the impulse to deny the gospel of civilization for the cult of Nature, which his religious persuasion should have made it difficult to do, or by his apprehension that the denial of Nature, so manifest all about him, was the beginning of still another end to man's apocalyptic hopes. That, of course, was the nub of his dilemma.

Cole joined the church fairly late in life and approached his subsequent work with a convert's zeal. Before he died he longed to repaint *The Course of Empire* as a Christian allegory. One can only wonder how he would have treated the series in these terms.

Marshall Davidson, a member of the advisory board of AMERICAN HERITAGE, *is editor of publications at the Metropolitan Museum of Art and author of a classic in the field of history as revealed by art,* Life In America, Houghton Mifflin, *1951.*

Doctor Gatling
and His Gun

CONTINUED FROM PAGE 51

in the rough country through which he had to travel. He also is said to have believed that the use of so devastating a weapon would cause him to lose face with the Indians.

Two years later, however, three Gatling guns were used in a battle against the Shoshones and Bannocks, who were in a seemingly impregnable position on top of a bluff near the Umatilla Agency. The Indians were quickly driven off the heights by the Gatlings' hail of bullets that swept along the crest and scattered the terrified warriors by their drumming rattle.

During the last part of the nineteenth century the Gatling's devastating firepower was tested many times against poorly armed natives in various parts of the world. During the Russo-Turkish War, a Captain Litvinoff, who operated one of his regiment's two guns, wrote what is perhaps the first account by an actual participant of the Gatling's deadly might. When a horde of howling Wyonoods made a surprise attack on the Russian camp in the middle of the night, the Captain described what happened:

"Though it was dark we perceived in front of us the galloping masses of the enemy with uplifted, glittering swords. When they approached us within about twenty paces I shouted the command 'Fire!' This was followed by a salvo of all men forming the cover and a simultaneous rattle of the two battery guns. In this roar the cries of the enemy at once became weak and then ceased altogether. . . . I ventured to get a look at the surrounding ground, availing myself of the first light of dawn. . . . At every step lay prostrated the dead bodies of the Wyonoods."

In 1879 the British used Gatlings against the Zulus, and in one encounter a single gun mowed down 473 tribesmen in a few minutes. And in 1882, when British troops invaded Egypt after the massacre of foreigners at Alexandria, 370 men armed with a few Gatlings captured and held the city while thousands of rioters and Egyptian troops were held back for four days, overawed by "the guns that pumped lead."

The definitive work on the subject is *The Machine Gun*, a four-volume work prepared for the Navy Bureau of Ordnance by Lieutenant Colonel George M. Chinn, lately of the Marine Corps. (Volumes two and three of this work are classified and not available to the public.) According to Colonel Chinn, machine guns have killed more people than any other mechanical device—including even the automobile—and the Maxim recoil movement alone has been responsible

TEXT CONTINUED ON PAGE 108

FROM *The Machine Gun*, BY GEORGE M. CHINN; BUREAU OF ORDNANCE, NAVY DEPARTMENT

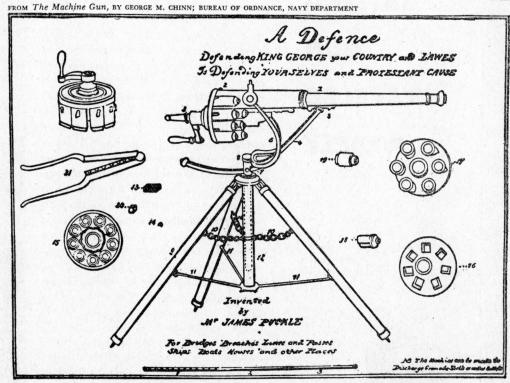

Square bullets for infidels and round ones for Christians were part of the world's first machine-gun patent, granted James Puckle by Britain in 1718.

THE GATLING GUN TRAVELED WIDELY

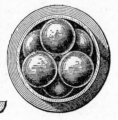

These cutaway drawings show the one-inch explosive shell used in later Gatlings, an effective anti-personnel weapon.

For more than a generation, the Gatling gun traveled the world and fought in many small wars. Thus there were many modifications of the design. In country too rough for other transport, for example, one could use the portable model shown above; it had ten barrels and upright magazines suspended from shoulder yokes. At the upper right is another variation, operating on the principle of the lawn mower, with the gun itself resting on a large steel caisson mounted on artillery wheels. It could be drawn by horses and quickly spun around by the man in the rear. The brass outer cover around the barrels was originally devised for use at sea, as a protection against corrosion. To the right is the famous camel gun designed for use in Egypt and the Orient, one of the most imaginative of all its applications. It was evidently designed to be fired by a man sitting in the saddle, but one may wonder whether a nervous camel could be trained to stand still while a violently recoiling, rip-snorting Gatling gun blasted away right over its ears. The same model also appears at the right on a portable tripod, while another is on a standard artillery carriage. In any form, the Gatling struck terror to the heart of the Fuzzy-Wuzzy and helped win many a colonial war.

for the death of more than 8,000,000 human beings. In the First World War, he says, 92 per cent of the casualties were caused by machine guns.

According to Colonel Chinn, the Gatling Gun Company sent trained operators abroad to stage demonstrations of the weapon. And, he says: "In their enthusiasm to put on a good show, they have been known to set up their guns against the enemy of a prospective customer and repel a charge, just to show its effectiveness as an instrument of annihilation."

It was during the Spanish-American War that Gatling guns first demonstrated their ability to win battles in which troops on both sides were equipped with modern weapons. The Spaniards had smokeless powder—something the American Army had not yet bothered to adopt because it had so much black powder on hand. As a result, Spanish marksmen could spot American soldiers each time they fired and then pick them off one by one. But even under such conditions, when their positions were revealed by clouds of smoke from the obsolete black powder, the Gatlings worked with the efficiency of riveting hammers.

Under the command of Lieutenant John H. Parker, the first soldier anywhere to appreciate the tactical power of machine guns in offensive warfare, four Gatling and two Colt machine guns were employed in the attack on Santiago, Cuba. Quick to pay tribute to the Gatlings' newly demonstrated value in such warfare was Lieutenant Colonel Theodore Roosevelt, who said: "The efficiency with which the Gatlings were handled by Parker was one of the most striking features of the campaign; he showed that a first-rate officer could use machine guns, on wheels, in battle and skirmish, in attacking and defending trenches, alongside of the best troops, and to their great advantage." After the war Parker wrote the first American machine-gun manual, which was published in 1899.

American armed forces were so neglected during the half century after 1865 that American-born inventors of military weapons could not find employment in their own country. One after another they went abroad to work for foreign governments. Yet nearly all the important machine-gun inventions were made by Americans.

In 1871 Benjamin B. Hotchkiss of Connecticut, working in France, developed a rapid-fire cannon which had revolving barrels turned by a crank like the Gatling gun. In 1884 Maine-born Hiram Stevens Maxim invented his widely used gun in England. This took advantage of the recoil of the barrel to do the loading and firing and so was the first completely automatic machine gun. Then, in the early 1890's, John Moses Browning of Utah invented an automatic weapon which made use of the discharge gases to operate the gun. Browning also spent much of his later life in Europe, for he lived and died in Belgium where his guns were manufactured.

These new automatic machine guns, many of them with single barrels cooled by a water jacket, made the manually operated Gatling seem out of date. In an effort to keep his invention alive, in 1893 Gatling developed an electric motor drive which fired his gun at the astounding rate of 3,000 rounds per minute. He also went on to build an automatic gas-operated gun, but by this time his product was meeting heavy competition throughout the world and was officially declared obsolete by the United States Army in 1911.

The Maxim recoil principle was used by all the nations engaged in the First World War. Mechanical technology in weapons design was then so far ahead of military thinking that in the early part of the war literally millions of men were slaughtered in senseless and hopeless frontal attacks against strongly held machine-gun positions. Then came several years of stalemate while the armies dug in. During this time new weapons were developed to attack troops protected by trenches and dugouts. Poison gas, tanks, and airplane bombs came into being while modern versions of old weapons like mortars and hand grenades were used to take machine-gun emplacements.

After more than half a century during which recoil and gas-operated machine guns dominated the military scene, a new and even more fearful weapon named the Vulcan was demonstrated at Maryland's Aberdeen Proving Ground in August, 1956. Its rate of fire is so rapid that it does not have the drumming effect of an ordinary machine gun, but, as one observer described it, sounds like the violent ripping of cloth. With the Vulcan, machine-gun development has completed a full circle, for the new gun is obviously patterned on Gatling's principle.

Both weapons have a rotating cluster of barrels and are externally powered. Long experience has shown that the multi-barreled system is easier to keep cool and that external power provides constant firing even if one barrel jams. Appropriately, the new Vulcan was first demonstrated alongside a Gatling gun. Now, more than sixty years after Gatling failed to convince the Army that his electric motor-driven gun was basically better than any recoil or gas-operated machine gun, the principles of the weapon he invented at the beginning of the Civil War are being used in our latest type of rapid-fire aircraft armament.

Philip Van Doren Stern, expert in such diverse fields as Lincoln, ordnance, and early automobiles, wrote "The Unknown Conspirator" for our February, 1957, issue.

Prescott's Conquests

CONTINUED FROM PAGE 8

crypt, his eyes were brushed by the coffin's drapes. "Yes," he sadly told Ticknor that evening, "my eye suffered very much from the wind and dust that came out of the passage, and *he* protected me to the last, as he always had." The historian himself had a deep fear of being mistakenly interred alive and ordered that at his death a principal vein be severed before his coffin was finally closed.

One may see these traits as the traumatic effects of his years of physical suffering and incapacitation, and find in his literary labors a compulsion to overcome frustration and weakness. But this is Prescott in a minor key—not the man of courage who nearly always presented his lighter side to his family and friends, who was unafraid to risk his crippled sight with each hour spent in reading or writing, and who could write wryly of himself to a Spanish friend, "As I have only half an eye of my own, and that more for show than use, my progress is necessarily no more than a snail's gallop."

Prescott never saw Spain or Latin America. His collection of manuscript copies—eight thousand folio pages for the *Conquest of Mexico* alone—he gathered in Europe entirely by proxy and by means of a vast correspondence, through friends or paid agents or from helpful foreign scholars. The historian Jared Sparks, Edward Everett, George Ticknor on his extensive Continental travels, and many others searched on Prescott's behalf into archives and libraries in half a dozen European nations.

Chief among his foreign collaborators was a Spanish scholar named Gayangos, whose perfect command of English and expert knowledge of Spanish history enabled him to serve Prescott superbly for twenty years. Prescott paid Gayangos' expenses for travel and copyists; beyond this the Spaniard would not go in accepting the compensation repeatedly offered by the American historian. Also important to Prescott's success in obtaining material from Spain was the cordial support given him by Fernández de Navarrete, president of the Royal Academy of History. Navarrete gave Prescott access to the academy's treasure of manuscripts and opened his own valuable collection to the scholar.

Little wonder that Prescott referred to Spain as "the country of my adoption," continuing, "I may truly call Spain so, for I have lived in it—in spirit at least—the last thirty years more of my time than in my own land." Spain was the land where "old manuscripts and old wines of the noblest kind flourish side by side—the land of the hidalgo—the land that I love."

The historian traveled seldom and reluctantly outside the tiny triangle of Boston, the North Shore, and Pepperell. Socially, too, he lived within close bounds. He and his wife were married in the same house where her parents had been wed. He lived at Harvard in the room where his father had lived, and where his own son would reside. Not one of the four houses in which he and his parents dwelt in Boston during his lifetime was more than a few hundred yards from the other or from Beacon Hill—when not on it.

Yet Prescott was an adventurer. Through his clouded eyes he saw the conquest of the New World, and he conveyed to his pages, for others to share, the excitement felt by conquistadors who penetrated the perilous kingdoms where no white man had ever been.

The Spanish conquests of Peru and Mexico were epics in fact. Prescott made them epics of literature. He recreated their unity of action, the brilliance of their settings, and the heroism and tragedy of their actors. He wrote of the conquest of Mexico in the introduction to his *Conquest of Peru:* "Indeed few subjects can present a parallel with that, for the purposes either of the historian or the poet. The natural development of the story, there, is precisely what would be prescribed by the severest rules of art. The conquest of the country is the great end always in view of the reader. From the first landing of the Spaniards on the soil, their subsequent adventures, their battles and negotiations, their ruinous retreat, their rally and final siege, all tend to this grand result, till the long series is closed by the downfall of the capital. In the march of events, all moves forward to this consummation. It is a magnificent epic, in which the unity of interest is complete."

Deeds of daring fill the pages: Cortés dismantling his ships (burning, Prescott incorrectly had it) on the mysterious shore of Mexico to forestall even the thought of retreat from the perils ahead; Pizarro sailing south from Panama along the unknown coast, and at last, in the face of disease, hunger, and death from the Indians, on an island off the coast of Ecuador, drawing a line in the sand from east to west with his sword and challenging his reluctant men to cross and continue onward with him: "There lies Peru with its riches; here, Panama and its poverty. Choose, each man, what best becomes a brave Castilian. For my part, I go to the south." Thirteen crossed, and by their boldness Spain gained yet another kingdom.

Here too are stories of a breed of men who amid the toil and peril of their march to Montezuma's capital turned aside out of sheer energy and curiosity to scale one of the world's highest volcanoes, Popocatepetl; men of whom it could be recorded as it was of each of the four brothers who led in the conquest of Peru: "To say that he was a Pizarro is enough to attest his claim to valor."

Not that Prescott's narratives are exclusively concerned with portraying the Spanish conquerors. He describes as well the Aztec and Peruvian Indians prior to the arrival of the white men. These parts of his work are fully as interesting as those dealing with the conquests, but they are historically less accurate.

The fault is not Prescott's. He employed all the sources known at the time when he wrote, he scrupulously analyzed and compared them, and he stated their limitations. His appraisals of the two greatest Indian civilizations of America have been considerably altered in detail by archeologists and anthropologists (whose interest Prescott was primarily responsible for awakening), although today's knowledge is far from complete. Yet his broad presentation of Aztec and Inca society remains valid. Although he tended to equate Indian institutions too readily with those of medieval and Renaissance Europe and perhaps to paint too romantic a picture of native life, his rugged

Prescott's noctograph

nineteenth-century liberalism was on guard, pointing to the defects of these societies as he saw them.

The Inca empire, for example, which in its economic organization approached an ideal agrarian communism and in its social and political organization was an admirably integrated hierarchy, may hold much charm for the twentieth-century reader, who will find it pictured in Prescott's pages as a stable regime of justice and security for all. But the author also had his own beliefs, which he did not hesitate to obtrude upon his readers: staunch confidence in representative government and belief in the inevitability of material and human progress, the whole founded upon faith in reason. He recognized the rule of the Inca, the emperor, for what it was—total rule.

"Where there is no free agency, there can be no morality," he continued with Lockean conviction, for "if that government is the best which is felt the least . . . then of all governments devised by man the Peruvian has the least real claim to our admiration." Nor did Prescott forbear to point up his assertions by

contrasting the Inca kingship and the government of the United States—"our own free republic" in which "the experiment still going on is humanity's best hope."

He also applied his liberal judgments to the Aztec empire. The fate of that confederacy, he wrote, "may serve as a striking proof that a government which does not rest on the sympathies of its subjects cannot long abide; that human institutions, when not connected with human prosperity and progress, must fall,—if not before the increasing light of civilization, by the hand of violence; by violence from within if not from without. And who shall lament their fall?"

Prescott's writings have defects of style and substance. Occasionally he confused and misattributed his Spanish manuscript sources. He did not understand the nature of the encomienda, the basic Spanish system for economic control of the Indians, which was not a method of land distribution but of tribute payment. His style is sometimes prolix and there are occasional digressions which detract from the main narrative. In general, however, he writes lucidly and powerfully, in a manner appropriate to the grand events which he relates. Read him, for example, on the meeting of the tiny Spanish army with the forces of one of the Aztec confederate nations: "The Spaniards had not advanced a quarter of a league when they came in sight of the Tlascalan army. Its dense array stretched far and wide over a vast plain or meadow ground, about six miles square. Its appearance justified the report which had been given of its numbers. Nothing could be more picturesque than the aspect of these Indian battalions, with the naked bodies of the common soldiers gaudily painted, the fantastic helmets of the chiefs glittering with gold and precious stones, and the glowing panoplies of featherwork which decorated their persons. Innumerable spears and darts tipped with points of transparent *itzli,* or fiery copper, sparkled bright in the morning sun, like the phosphoric gleams playing on the surface of a troubled sea, while the rear of the mighty host was dark with the shadows of banners, on which were emblazoned the armorial bearings of the Tlascalan and Otomie chiefs."

Prescott was stylist and historian in superb combination. Notwithstanding what he termed the "seductions" of his subjects, his standard of accuracy and his objective were never lowered. He wrote: "I have conscientiously endeavored to distinguish fact from fiction, and to establish the narrative on as broad a basis as possible of contemporary evidence." The task of the historian, in his opinion, was "to fill up the outline with the coloring of life," yet "to place the whole on the foundation of copious citations from the original authorities." His integrity to his sources was as complete as he could make it. If the ultimate synthesis was his own, so it must be with all written history that is more than a lumpish assortment of data. His endeavor was one of the highest and most difficult for a historian to fulfill; he strove to make his reader "a contemporary of the sixteenth century"—in the raw New World, he might have added.

He heavily discounted the long-accepted but exaggerated accounts of the destruction worked upon the Indian populations by the Spanish conquerors and colonists. It was on the basis of these accounts, further embellished, that other European powers, especially the English, served their own imperial ambitions by constructing the "black legend" of the Spanish conquest and settlement of America. Yet Prescott made no saints of the Spanish soldiers. He contrasted their spiritual claims and their temporal objectives with an irony as biting as that of Gibbon in his judgments on early Christianity.

Were the Spaniards hypocrites? Prescott thought not. "Whatever the vices of the Castilian cavalier, hypocrisy was not among the number. He felt that he was battling for the Cross, and under this conviction . . . he was blind to the baser motives that mingled in the enterprise."

Prescott denounced the Inquisition (here the historian's own sentiments led him into a mild distortion of the facts, for the Inquisition as a formal tribunal was not introduced into the Indies until a later time) and denounced it so severely that Aztec human sacrifices seem more acceptable to him than some of the acts of the churchmen. None the less, he applauded the missionary work of the priests, many of whom "were men of singular humility, who followed in the track of the conquerors to scatter the seeds of spiritual truth." The conquistadors did evil, but they "also brought Christianity, whose benign influence would still survive when the fierce flames of fanaticism should be extinguished."

He also pointed out a fact about his own religious and national inheritance: "The effort to Christianize the heathen is an honorable characteristic of the Spanish conquerors. The Puritan, with equal religious zeal, did comparatively little for the conversion of the Indians."

Within the context of ideas and the condition of historical studies in the United States in the first half of the past century, Prescott stands out as a mighty pioneer. Lacking a native historical tradition and technique, lacking the libraries and bibliographies available to scholars who followed him, his path was additionally beset by personal obstacles. Despite all this,

his narratives of two of mankind's most daring military conquests must still be awarded the historian's highest accolade: they are definitive. More readable and accurate than Sparks, more productive than Motley, more objective than Bancroft, Prescott has but one peer among American historians, Parkman, who also suffered severely from physical disability.

Prescott's books share the nature of the granite edifices of the Incas which he describes in the *Conquest of Peru*: they are massive creations of a master craftsman, handsomely and tightly contrived. With time's passage a few stones have become dislodged or chipped, but the structure stands firm, perhaps forever.

It was dedication and hard work that won Prescott mastery of his profession and of himself. This may be seen even in the small, amusing details of his self-discipline, for example, in his standing order that on cold mornings, did he not arise promptly upon being called, his manservant should pull the covers from his bed. It may be seen at the long, late parties where he always fixed for himself an early hour of departure and held to it.

This Bostonian had much of the Spaniard in him. He was gay, yet dignified, even austere; often indolent, yet even more often energetic; willful and courageous. But his tempered New England conscience was the impelling force in his life, driving him to hard work ruled by high standards. The adventurer living on the edge of darkness triumphed over the sociable literary dilettante. He gained another victory which his fellow Americans understood and admired: he capitalized his principle by investing his inherited wealth in books and manuscripts and labor, and constructing from these materials a national and international reputation greater than that of any of his business or lawyer friends.

Prescott did more. He was one of the first to set out on the then untraveled roads between the United States and Spain and Latin America; by his efforts our country today is closer to these nations.

One hundred years ago his books were read for their fine style and somewhat later, with the development of historical studies, they were recognized as superb history. Having passed both tests, after ten decades, he continues to attract new readers, who seek him out as a master craftsman of American literature. And behind the books stands the man, for Prescott's conquests were not two, but three: the third, and perhaps the greatest, was his own life.

Thomas F. McGann is an assistant professor of history at Harvard and specializes in Latin America. He has spent 1956-57 in Spain doing archival research for a study of the Spanish empire in America.

George Washington's
Great-Great-Great-
Great-Great-Grandfather Slept Here

In 1539 the former mayor of the town of Northampton, England, a prosperous wool merchant named Lawrence Washington (the great-great-great-great-great-grandfather of George Washington) settled north of Oxford in the hill country known as the Cotswolds. There he built a handsome stone cottage for himself and his large family which he called Sulgrave Manor. Part of a monastic estate confiscated by King Henry VIII when he broke with the Church of Rome five years earlier, it was situated in pleasant farm country where ancient lanes wandered for miles between wild rose hedges (which sometimes concealed highwaymen), and certain lonely barrows were reputed to be gathering places for local witches. This was a region where Nonconformist sects gained an early foothold, and the Puritanic tendencies of the natives were proverbial.

The two panels of heraldic stained glass which adorn the front and back covers of this issue were originally at Sulgrave Manor. This spring they were sold by their owner, British author Sacheverell Sitwell, to the Corning Museum of Glass in Corning, New York, where they are now on permanent display. Of seven related panels, these are the only ones which have come to George Washington's native country.

Both panels shown here were probably made in 1588, the year Queen Elizabeth's Navy and the storms which Spaniards called "Protestant winds" destroyed the great Armada. The panels commemorate two marriages in the Washington family, one of them bearing the coat of arms of John Washington and Margaret Kytson, and the other, the arms of Margaret Butler and a second Lawrence Washington, the grandson of the builder of Sulgrave Manor.

The Washington coat of arms has a pattern of red and white bars and three five-pointed stars—or, in more heraldic language, "Argent, Two Bars Gules, in Chief Three Mullets of the Second." Some historians have made the perhaps romantic assertion that these Washington arms were the original inspiration for the national flag of the United States which the Continental Congress adopted on June 14, 1777.

Apparently the Washington family fortune diminished in the years after the panels were made, for in 1610 Sulgrave Manor had to be sold. Almost fifty years later the first Washington arrived in the New World. In 1657—the last year of Oliver Cromwell's Puritan dictatorship in England—George Washington's great-grandfather John sailed to Virginia as first mate and part owner of a trading ketch. When his ship was wrecked on a Rappahannock River shoal, John Washington elected to remain in America. The prospect of plentiful tobacco land was inviting; and, too, he must have been happy to settle beyond the stern reach of a Puritan-dominated England. For John Washington had seen his clergyman father ruined by the Puritans, who had branded him as a "common frequenter of ale houses" and ousted him from his parish.

As the Washington name became famous, Sulgrave Manor fell upon hard times. One wing was demolished in the eighteenth century; and when Washington Irving visited early in the 1850's, he could report that "A part only of the manor house remained and was inhabited by a farmer." While at Sulgrave, Irving also viewed some of the heraldic panels. "The Washington crest, in colored glass, was to be seen in a window of what was now the buttery," he wrote. "A window on which the whole family arms was emblazoned had been removed to the residence of the actual proprietor of the manor."

The latter were evidently the same panels which came into the hands of the Sitwell family when it purchased Sulgrave Manor at this time. Recently, Sacheverell Sitwell related that when his great-grandfather bought the house, he seemed to have some inkling of the potential historical value of the panels, for he had them removed from their place in the hall and enclosed in a wooden box.

This year two of the Washington panels were brought to America. Five more originals remain in England, and facsimiles of all seven may be seen in Sulgrave Manor, which was purchased in 1914 by the British Committee for the Celebration of 100 Years of Peace between Britain and America and restored to its original condition.